SHAKESPEARE MADE EASY

Modern version side-by-side with full original text

Henry IV
Part One

Edited and rendered into modern English by
Alan Durband

Hutchinson

London   Melbourne   Sydney   Auckland   Johannesburg

Hutchinson and Co. (Publishers) Ltd
An imprint of the Hutchinson Publishing Group
17–21 Conway Street, London W1P 6JD

Hutchinson Publishing Group (Australia) Pty Ltd
PO Box 496, 16–22 Church Street, Hawthorn, Melbourne,
  Victoria 3122

Hutchinson Group (NZ) Ltd
32–34 View Road, PO Box 40–086, Glenfield, Auckland 10

Hutchinson Group (SA) (Pty) Ltd
PO Box 337, Bergvlei 2012, South Africa

First published 1984
© Alan Durband 1984

Set in 10/12pt Plantin & Univers by Colset Pte Ltd, Singapore

Made and printed in Great Britain by the
Guernsey Press Co. Ltd., Guernsey, Channel Islands.

British Library Cataloguing in Publication Data

Shakespeare, William
  Henry IV Part One
  I. Title   II. Durband, Alan   III. Series
  822.3'3   PR2810

ISBN 0 09 940130 4 (UK edition)

ISBN 0 09 156431 X (export edition)

'*Reade him, therefore; and againe, and againe: And if then you do not like him, surely you are in some danger, not to understand him. . . .*'

John   Hemming
Henry Condell

Preface to the 1623 Folio Edition

Shakespeare Made Easy

Titles in the series

Macbeth
Julius Caesar
Merchant of Venice
Romeo and Juliet
Henry IV Part One
A Midsummer Night's Dream

Other drama books edited by Alan Durband:

Contents

Introduction

Shakespeare Made Easy is intended for readers approaching the plays for the first time, who find the language of Elizabethan poetic drama an initial obstacle to understanding and enjoyment. In the past, the only answer to the problem has been to grapple with the difficulties with the aid of explanatory footnotes (often missing when they are most needed) and a stern teacher. Generations of students have complained that 'Shakespeare was ruined for me at school'.

Usually a fuller appreciation of Shakespeare's plays comes in later life, when the mind has matured and language skills are more developed. Often the desire to read Shakespeare for pleasure and enrichment follows from a visit to the theatre, where excellence of acting and production can bring to life qualities which sometimes lie dormant on the printed page.

Shakespeare Made Easy can never be a substitute for the original plays. It cannot possibly convey the full meaning of Shakespeare's poetic expression, which is untranslatable. *Shakespeare Made Easy* concentrates on the dramatic aspect, enabling the novice to become familiar with the plot and characters, and to experience one facet of Shakespeare's genius. To know and understand the central issues of each play is a sound starting point for further exploration and development.

Discretion can be used in choosing the best method to employ. One way is to read the original Shakespeare first, ignoring the modern translation or using it only when interest or understanding flags. Another way is to read the translation first, to establish confidence and familiarity with plots and characters.

Either way, cross-reference can be illuminating. The modern text can explain 'what is being said' if Shakespeare's language is particularly complex or his expression antiquated. The

Shakespeare text will show the reader of the modern paraphrase how much more can be expressed in poetry than in prose.

The use of *Shakespeare Made Easy* means that the newcomer need never be overcome by textual difficulties. From first to last, a measure of understanding is at hand – the key is provided for what has been a locked door to many students in the past. And as understanding grows, so an awareness develops of the potential of language as a vehicle for philosophic and moral expression, beauty, and the abidingly memorable.

Even professional Shakespearian scholars can never hope to arrive at a complete understanding of the plays. Each critic, researcher, actor or producer merely adds a little to the work that has already been done, or makes fresh interpretations of the texts for new generations. For everyone, Shakespearian appreciation is a journey. *Shakespeare Made Easy* is intended to help with the first steps.

William Shakespeare

His life

William Shakespeare was born in Stratford-on-Avon, Warwick-shire, on 23 April 1564, the son of a prosperous wool and lea-ther merchant. Very little is known of his early life. From parish records we know that he married Ann Hathaway in 1582, when he was eighteen, and she was twenty-six. They had three children, the eldest of whom died in childhood.

Between his marriage and the next thing we know about him, there is a gap of ten years. Probably he became a member of a travelling company of actors. By 1592 he had settled in London, and had earned a reputation as an actor and playwright.

Theatres were then in their infancy. The first (called *The Theatre*) was built by the actor James Burbage in 1576, in Shoreditch, then a suburb of London. Two more followed as the taste for theatre grew: *The Curtain* in 1577 and *The Rose* in 1587. The demand for new plays naturally increased. Shakespeare probably earned a living adapting old plays and working in collaboration with others on new ones. Today we would call him a 'freelance', since he was not permanently attached to one theatre.

In 1594, a new company of actors, The Lord Chamberlain's Men was formed, and Shakespeare was one of the shareholders. He remained a member throughout his working life. The Com-pany was grouped in 1603, and re-named The King's Men, with James I as their patron.

Shakespeare and his fellow-actors prospered. In 1598 they built their own theatre, *The Globe*, which broke away from the traditional rectangular shape of the inn and its yard (the early home of travelling bands of actors). Shakespeare described it in *Henry V* as 'this wooden O', because it was circular.

Many other theatres were built by investors eager to profit from the new enthusiasm for drama. *The Hope*, *The Fortune*, *The Red Bull*, and *The Swan* were all open-air 'public' theatres. There were also many 'private' (or indoor) theatres, one of which (*The Blackfriars*) was purchased by Shakespeare and his friends because the child actors who performed there were dangerous competitors (Shakespeare denounces them in *Hamlet*).

After writing some thirty-seven plays (the exact number is something which scholars argue about), Shakespeare retired to his native Stratford, wealthy and respected. He died on his birthday, in 1616.

His plays

Shakespeare's plays were not all published in his lifetime. None of them comes to us exactly as he wrote it.

In Elizabethan times, plays were not regarded as either litera-ture or good reading matter. They were written at speed (often by more than one writer), performed perhaps ten or twelve times, and then discarded. Fourteen of Shakespeare's plays were first printed in Quarto (17cm × 21cm) volumes, not all with his name as the author. Some were authorized (the 'good' Quartos) and probably were printed from prompt copies pro-vided by the theatre. Others were pirated (the 'bad' Quartos) by booksellers who may have employed shorthand writers, or bought actors' copies after the run of the play had ended.

In 1623, seven years after Shakespeare's death, John Hemming and Henry Condell (fellow-actors and share-holders in The King's Men) published a collected edition of Shakespeare's works – thirty-six plays in all – in a Folio (21cm × 34cm) edition. From their introduction it would seem that they used Shakespeare's original manuscripts ('we have scarce received from him a blot in his papers') but the Folio volumes that still survive are not all exactly alike, nor are the plays printed as we know them today, with act and scene divisions and stage-directions.

A modern edition of a Shakespeare play is the result of a great deal of scholarly research and editorial skill over several centuries. The aim is always to publish a text (based on the good and bad Quartos and the Folio editions) that most closely resembles what Shakespeare intended. Misprints have added to the problems, so some words and lines are pure guesswork. This explains why some versions of Shakespeare's plays differ from others.

His theatre

The first purpose-built playhouse in Elizabethan London, constructed in 1576, was *The Theatre*. Its co-founders were John Brayne, an investor, and James Burbage, a carpenter turned actor. Like the six or seven 'public' (or outdoor) theatres which followed it over the next thirty years, it was situated outside the city, to avoid conflict with the authorities. They disapproved of players and playgoing, partly on moral and political grounds, and partly because of the danger of spreading the plague. (There were two major epidemics during Shakespeare's lifetime, and on each occasion the theatres were closed for lengthy periods.)

The Theatre was a financial success, and Shakespeare's company performed there until 1598, when a dispute over the lease of the land forced Burbage to take down the building. It was re-created in Southwark, as *The Globe*, with Shakespeare and several of his fellow-actors as the principal shareholders.

By modern standards, *The Globe* was small. Externally, the octagonal building measured less than thirty metres across, but in spite of this it could accommodate an audience of between two and three thousand people. (The largest of the three theatres at the National Theatre complex in London today seats 1160.)

Performances were advertised by means of playbills posted around the city, and they took place during the hours of day-

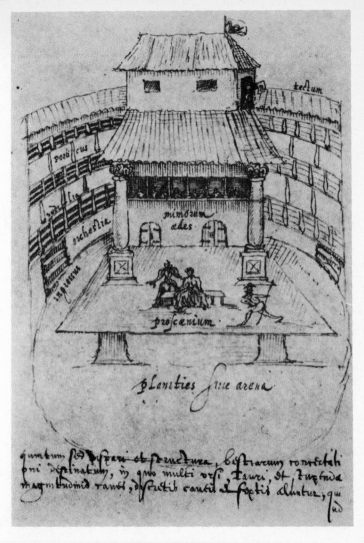

Interior of the Swan Theatre – from a pen and ink drawing made in 1596 (Mansell Collection)

light when the weather was suitable. A flag flew to show that all was well, to save playgoers a wasted journey.

At the entrance, a doorkeeper collected one penny (about 60p in modern money) for admission to the 'pit' – a name taken from the old inn-yards, where bear-baiting and cock-fighting were popular sports. This was the minimum charge for seeing a play. The 'groundlings', as they were called, simply stood around the three sides of the stage, in the open air. Those who were better off could pay extra for a seat under cover. Stairs led from the pit to three tiers of galleries round the walls. The higher one went, the more one paid. The best seats cost one shilling, (or £6 today). In theatres owned by speculators like Francis Langley and Philip Henslowe, half the gallery takings went to the landlord.

A full house might consist of 800 groundlings and 1500 in the galleries, with a dozen more exclusive seats on the stage itself for the gentry. A new play might run for between six and sixteen performances; the average was about ten. As there were no breaks between scenes, and no intervals, most plays could be performed in two hours. A trumpet sounded three times before the play began.

The acting company assembled in the Tiring House at the rear of the stage. This was where they 'attired' (or dressed) themselves: not in costumes representing the period of the play, but in Elizabethan doublet and hose. All performances were therefore in modern dress, though no expense was spared to make the stage costumes lavish. The entire company was male. By law actresses were not allowed, and female roles were performed by boys.

Access to the stage from the Tiring House was through two doors, one on each side of the stage. Because there was no front curtain, every entrance had to have its corresponding exit, so an actor killed on stage had to be carried off. There was no scenery: the audience used its imagination, guided by the spoken word. Storms and night scenes might well be performed on sunny days in mid-afternoon; the Elizabethan playgoer relied entirely on the playwrights' descriptive skills to establish the dramatic atmosphere.

Once on stage, the actors and their expensive clothes were protected from sudden showers by a canopy, the underside of which was painted blue, and spangled with stars to represent the heavens. A trapdoor in the stage made ghostly entrances and the gravedigging scene in *Hamlet* possible. Behind the main stage, in between the two entrance doors, there was a curtained area, concealing a small inner stage, useful for bedroom scenes. Above this was a balcony, which served for castle walls (as in *Henry V*) or a domestic balcony (as in the famous scene in *Romeo and Juliet*).

The acting style in Elizabethan times was probably more declamatory than we favour today, but the close proximity of the audience also made a degree of intimacy possible. In those days soliloquies and asides seemed quite natural. Act and scene divisions did not exist (those in printed versions of the play today have been added by editors), but Shakespeare often indicates a scene-ending by a rhyming couplet.

A company such as The King's Men at *The Globe* would consist of around twenty-five actors, half of whom might be shareholders, and the rest part-timers engaged for a particular play. Amongst the shareholders in *The Globe* were several specialists – William Kempe, for example, was a renowned comedian and Robert Armin was a singer and dancer. Playwrights wrote parts to suit the actors who were available, and devised ways of overcoming the absence of women. Shakespeare often has his heroines dress as young men, and physical contact between lovers was formal compared with the realism we expect today.

His verse

Shakespeare wrote his plays mostly in blank verse: that is,

unrhymed lines consisting of ten syllables, alternately stressed and unstressed. The technical term for this form is the 'iambic pentameter'. When Shakespeare first began to write for the stage, it was fashionable to maintain this regular beat from the first line of the play till the last.

Shakespeare conformed at first, and then experimented. Some of his early plays contain whole scenes in rhyming couplets – in *Romeo and Juliet*, for example, there is extensive use of rhyme, and as if to show his versatility, Shakespeare even inserts a sonnet into the dialogue.

But as he matured, he sought greater freedom of expression than rhyme allowed. Rhyme is still used to indicate a scene-ending, or to stress lines which he wishes the audience to remember. Generally, though, Shakespeare moved towards the rhythms of everyday speech. This gave him many dramatic advantages, which he fully and subtly exploits in terms of atmosphere, character, emotion, stress and pace.

It is Shakespeare's poetic imagery, however, that most distinguishes his verse from that of lesser playwrights. It enables him to stretch the imagination, express complex thought-patterns in memorable language, and convey a number of associated ideas in a compressed and economical form. A study of Shakespeare's imagery – especially in his later plays – is often the key to a full understanding of his meaning and purposes.

At the other extreme is prose. Shakespeare normally reserves it for servants, clowns, commoners, and pedestrian matters such as lists, messages and letters.

Henry IV Part One

Date

Henry IV Part One was probably written in 1596–7. It was first entered in the Stationer's Register in 1598, and first printed in the same year, in a Quarto edition published by Peter Short. The Folio edition of 1623 was set up from the fifth edition of the Quarto.

Source

Shakespeare's historical material mostly comes from Ralph Holinshed's *Chronicles of England, Scotland and Ireland*, first published in 1577 and reprinted ten years later.

Shakespeare takes considerable liberties with the facts, to suit his dramatic purposes. Prince Hal and Hotspur are the same age, though in reality the former was sixteen, whereas the latter was in his late thirties and two years older than the King. Prince John was only thirteen at the time of the Battle of Shrewsbury, and there is no historical evidence that he took part in it.

Shakespeare also juggles with chronology. The reconciliation between the Prince and King Henry took place later in history than it does in the play. Plans for the crusade were discussed at the end of Henry's reign, not at the beginning.

Characters are confused: for example there were two historical Edmund Mortimers, and Shakespeare mixes them up. The one who was Hotspur's brother-in-law was not the Mortimer named by King Richard as his heir. Other characters are given qualities they did not have – Shakespeare invents the heroic deeds of the Prince in the Battle of Shrewsbury, and makes Henry more magnanimous towards the defeated than he really was. He suppresses the fact that Hotspur's dead body was crushed and mutilated after victory, as an act of revenge. Falstaff and the low-life characters are, of course, entirely original.

Other source material has been traced. Samuel Daniel's poem published in 1595, *'The first four books of the civil wars between the two houses of Lancaster and York'*, must have been at Shakespeare's side, since many of his historical interpretations (and errors) are incorporated in the play. So too must John Stow's *Chronicles of England* (1580) and *Annals of England* (1592). There are several details in the two books which coincide with Shakespeare's version of history.

Shakespeare also drew upon existing plays; it was a common Elizabethan practice in the theatre to re-work old material. There were several relevant texts in circulation, none of any literary merit. The play with the closest resemblance – the anonymous *Famous Victories of Henry the Fifth* – was first entered in the Stationer's Register of 1594, and was probably itself a re-write of other plays dealing with the same historical period. In this play there is a Sir John Oldcastle, far removed from Shakespeare's character Falstaff, but undoutedly in his mind when he wrote *Henry IV Part One*. There is clear evidence that he used the name Oldcastle in his early draft of the play, changing it to Falstaff after protests from Oldcastle's descendants.

The historical background

In 1389, Richard II decided to rule the kingdom without the Council that had advised him since he was ten years old. He became very powerful, and his court was famous for its magnificence.

By 1398 Richard was in a very strong position. He dealt with his enemies ruthlessly, having them murdered, executed and banished. Many of his subjects felt threatened and one, Thomas Mowbray (Duke of Norfolk), fearing for his safety, expressed his concern to Henry Bolingbroke (son of the respected John of Gaunt, Duke of Lancaster and uncle of the king). Bolingbroke reported Mowbray's traitorous remarks to Richard.

Richard summoned both men to court. After hearing their evidence, he decided that Bolingbroke and Mowbray should fight the matter out in mortal combat. But on the appointed day, Richard changed his mind. He sentenced both men to banishment, Bolingbroke for ten years and Mowbray for life.

Thinking he had rid himself of two dangerous men, Richard felt even more secure. So when John of Gaunt died early the following year (1399) he acted swiftly. He seized Gaunt's estates, and extended Bolingbroke's banishment to life. A few months later, supremely self-confident, he left for Ireland with a large army and most of his supporters, intending to solve a problem that had troubled England for many years.

But Richard had alienated many of the nobles. They were afraid of losing their own property and rights. Knowing that he would be well supported, Henry Bolingbroke took advantage of this opportunity. He returned home to claim his inheritance. He landed at Ravenspur in Yorkshire in July 1399. He was met by the Earl of Northumberland (surnamed Percy) and later by the Earl's son, Hotspur. He assured the Percys that his objective was merely to recover his lands and the Dukedom of Lancaster, and that no harm was meant to the King. The common people hailed Bolingbroke as a popular hero, and he marched through England in triumph, meeting no resistance.

Richard was naturally alarmed. He returned at once from Ireland to defend his rights as the anointed king. But, hated and friendless, he was soon captured by Bolingbroke, and held prisoner.

The nobles decided to offer the crown to Bolingbroke, and he accepted it. Now, Richard was too dangerous to live. He was secretly murdered and buried in an obscure grave.

Henry IV's reign was a troubled one from its earliest days. He lived in constant fear of rebellions led by nobles who disputed his right to the throne.

In *Henry IV Part One* Henry's main enemies are Mortimer, who had a claim to the throne through the female line, Glendower, a Welsh chieftain whose daughter was married to Mortimer, and the Percys, who, having fought for Henry against the Scots, felt badly treated by him.

Text

The text as we know it today can be traced back directly to the first Quarto of 1598. The editors of the Folio Edition added act and scene divisions, which was unusual at that time.

Henry IV
Part One

Original text and modern version

The characters

King Henry the Fourth
Henry Prince of Wales ⎫
Lord John of Lancaster ⎬ The King's sons
⎭
Earl of Westmoreland
Sir Walter Blunt
Thomas Percy Earl of Worcester
Henry Percy Earl of Northumberland
Henry Percy (Hotspur) his son
Edmund Mortimer Earl of March
Archibald Earl of Douglas
Owen Glendower
Sir Richard Vernon
Richard Scroop Archbishop of York
Sir Michael a friend of the Archbishop of York
Sir John Falstaff
Poins
Peto
Bardolph
Gadshill
Francis a waiter
Lady Percy Hotspur's wife and Mortimer's sister
Lady Mortimer Glendower's daughter and Mortimer's wife
Mistress Quickly hostess of the Boar's Head in Eastcheap
Lords, Sheriff, Vintner, Chamberlain, Waiters, two **Carriers, Ostler, Messengers, Travellers,** and **Attendants**

Act one

Scene 1

London. The Palace. Enter the **King, Lord John of Lancaster, Earl of Westmoreland, Sir Walter Blunt** *with others.*

King So shaken as we are, so wan with care,
Find we a time for frighted peace to pant,
And breathe short-winded accents of new broils
To be commenced in stronds afar remote.
5 No more the thirsty entrance of this soil
Shall daub her lips with her own children's blood,
No more shall trenching war channel her fields,
Nor bruise her flow'rets with the armed hoofs
Of hostile paces: those opposed eyes,
10 Which, like the meteors of a troubled heaven,
All of one nature, or one substance bred,
Did lately meet in the intestine shock
And furious close of civil butchery,
Shall now, in mutual well-beseeming ranks,
15 March all one way, and be no more opposed
Against acquaintance, kindred, and allies.
The edge of war, like an ill-sheathed knife,
No more shall cut his master. Therefore, friends,
As far as to the sepulchre of Christ –
20 Whose soldier now, under whose blessed cross
We are impressed and engaged to fight –
Forthwith a power of English shall we levy,
Whose arms were moulded in their mothers' womb
To chase these pagans in those holy field
25 Over whose acres walked those blessed feet

Act one

Scene 1

The King's palace in London, 1402. Enter **King Henry IV,
Lord John of Lancaster,** *the* **Earl of Westmoreland, Sir
Walter Blunt,** *and others*

King [*addressing the assembled court*] War-weary and
exhausted as we are, let's give frightened peace an
opportunity to recover her breath. Then, while she's still
panting, we'll announce a Crusade to be fought in the
distant holy lands. No longer shall we water our native
soil with the blood of our fellow-countrymen. There'll be
no more trenches cut through our fields; no more tender
crops trampled beneath the hooves of charging cavalry.
Men who clashed in civil war, slaughtering each other in
close combat, their eyes flashing like meteors in a stormy
sky, yet all of common stock, will now line up together in
orderly ranks, marching in the same direction, no more at
odds with friends, relations, and former allies. No longer
shall war injure those who wage it, like the sharp edge of
a knife that's badly sheathed. Therefore, friends, Christ's
soldiers as we are, conscripts of the blessed cross, we'll
raise an army bound for Jerusalem. Every Englishman is
born to serve the cause of driving out the pagans from
the holy fields, over which those blessed feet, nailed to

Which fourteen hundred years ago were nailed
For our advantage on the bitter cross.
But this our purpose now is twelve month old,
And bootless 'tis to tell you we will go;
30   Therefore we meet not now. Then let me hear
Of you, my gentle cousin Westmoreland,
What yesternight our Council did decree
In forwarding this dear expedience.

Westmoreland My liege, this haste was hot in question,
35   And many limits of the charge set down
But yesternight, when all athwart there came
A post from Wales, loaden with heavy news,
Whose worst was that the noble Mortimer,
Leading the men of Herefordshire to fight
40   Against the irregular and wild Glendower,
Was by the rude hands of that Welshman taken,
A thousand of his people butchered,
Upon whose dead corpse there was such misuse,
Such beastly shameless transformation,
45   By those Welshwomen done, as may not be
Without much shame retold or spoken of.

King It seems then that the tidings of this broil
Brake off our business for the Holy Land.

Westmoreland This matched with other did, my gracious
    lord,
50   For more uneven and unwelcome news
Came from the north, and thus it did import:
On Holy-rood day, the gallant Hotspur there,
Young Harry Percy, and brave Archibald,
That ever valiant and approved Scot,
55   At Holmedon met, where they did spend
A sad and bloody hour;
As by discharge of their artillery,
And shape of likelihood, the news was told;

the cross for our sakes fourteen hundred years ago, once walked. A year has passed since we resolved on this, and I needn't stress that we shall go; that's not the issue. So, my dear kinsman Westmoreland, tell me what the Council proposed last night in pursuit of this cherished ambition.

Westmoreland   My liege, this top priority was discussed enthusiastically, and many detailed strategies were planned during the evening. But cutting right across all this, a messenger came from Wales bearing bad news. The worst was that noble Mortimer, leading a troop of Hertfordshire men against the guerrilla fighter Owen Glendower, was captured by that Welsh bandit. A thousand of his men were massacred. The appalling mutilations inflicted on the corpses by those Welshwomen are better not described.

King   It would seem, then, that we must put off our plans for the holy land, now that we've had news of this engagement.

Westmoreland   That and other things, my gracious lord. Even more disturbing and unwelcome news came from the North, to this effect: on 14 September, the gallant Hotspur (young Harry Percy) and brave Archibald (that ever-valiant and respected Scot, the Earl of Douglas) met at Holmedon in Northumberland where they fought a bloody battle, according to reports of the encounter and

For he that brought them, in the very heat
60   And pride of their contention did take horse,
Uncertain of the issue any way.

King   Here is a dear, a true industrious friend,
Sir Walter Blunt, new lighted from his horse,
Stained with the variation of each soil
65   Betwixt that Holmedon and this seat of ours;
And he hath brought us smooth and welcome news.
The Earl of Douglas is discomfited;
Ten thousand bold Scots, two and twenty knights,
Balked in their own blood, did Sir Walter see
70   On Holmedon's plains; of prisoners Hotspur took
Mordake, Earl of Fife and eldest son
To beaten Douglas, and the Earl of Athol,
Of Murray, Angus, and Menteith:
And is not this an honourable spoil?
75   A gallant prize? Ha, cousin, is it not?

Westmoreland   In faith,
It is a conquest for a prince to boast of.

King   Yea, there thou mak'st me sad, and mak'st me sin
In envy that my Lord Northumberland
Should be the father to so blest a son;
80   A son who is the theme of honour's tongue,
Amongst a grove the very straightest plant,
Who is sweet Fortune's minion and her pride;
Whilst I by looking on the praise of him
See riot and dishonour stain the brow
85   Of my young Harry. O that it could be proved
That some night-tripping fairy had exchanged
In cradle-clothes our children where they lay,
And called mine Percy, his Plantagenet!
Then would I have his Harry, and he mine:
90   But let him from my thoughts. What think you, coz,

the subsequent events. The messenger galloped off at the height of the struggle, not knowing what the outcome was either way.

King   [*pointing to a travel-weary knight*] Here is a dear, loyal, and zealous friend, Sir Walter Blunt, covered in every variety of dust to be found between the palace here and Holmedon. He has brought us good and welcome news. The Earl of Douglas has been beaten. Sir Walter saw ten thousand brawny Scots, and twenty-two knights, lying defeated in bloodsoaked ruts in Holmedon's fields. Hotspur took Mordake, the Earl of Fife (and eldest son of the vanquished Douglas) prisoner, and also the Earls of Athol, Murray, Angus and Mentieth. Isn't this very honourable booty? A gallant prize, eh, cousin? Is it not?

Westmoreland   Indeed, it is a conquest that a prince could boast of.

King   [*his face clouding*] Yes, and there you trouble me. I'm sinfully envious that Lord Northumberland should be the father of a son so blessed. A son whom Honour is for ever praising. The straightest tree in any wood. The pride and joy of Fortune. In comparison with Hotspur's praiseworthy qualities, I see brawling and discreditable behaviour spoiling the reputation of my young Harry. I wish it could be proved that one night a fairy exchanged our children as they lay in their cradles, and called mine Harry Percy, and his Harry Plantagenet! Then I'd have his Harry, and he'd have mine. [*Pulling himself together*] But

Of this young Percy's pride? The prisoners
Which he in this adventure hath surprised
To his own use he keeps, and sends me word
I shall have none but Mordake, Earl of Fife.

95 **Westmoreland**   This is his uncle's teaching, this is
        Worcester,
Malevolent to you in all aspects,
Which makes him prune himself, and bristle up
The crest of youth against your dignity.

100 **King**   But I have sent for him to answer this;
And for this cause awhile we must neglect
Our holy purpose to Jerusalem.
Cousin, on Wednesday next our Council we
Will hold at Windsor, so inform the lords:
But come yourself with speed to us again,
105 For more is to be said and to be done
Than out of anger can be uttered.

Westmoreland   I will, my liege.

[*Exeunt*]

Scene 2

London. An apartment of the Prince's. Enter the **Prince of Wales** *and* **Sir John Falstaff**

Falstaff   Now, Hal, what time of day is it, lad?

Prince   Thou art so fat-witted with drinking of old sack,
and unbuttoning thee after supper, and sleeping upon
benches after noon, that thou hast forgotten to demand

I mustn't talk of him. [*To* **Westmoreland**] What do
you make of this young Percy's arrogance, cousin? He's
keeping the prisoners he took for his own purposes,
sending me word I can only have Mordake, the Earl of
Fife!

Westmoreland   His uncle has put him up to this: this is
Worcester's work. He thwarts you in every possible way.
He preens himself, and stirs young people up against
your authority.

King   I've sent for him to answer for this. For this reason,
we must postpone our holy plan to go to Jerusalem.
Cousin, tell the Lords we'll hold our Council at Windsor
next Wednesday. Then return to me at once. There's
more to be said and done than should be said in public,
given my present angry mood.

Westmoreland   I will, my liege.

[*They go*]

Scene 2

The Prince's apartment in London. **Falstaff** *is asleep. The*
Prince of Wales *tickles his nose till he wakes*

Falstaff   Now Hal – what's the time, lad?

Prince   You're so thick-headed with drinking that sherry,
and unfastening your buttons after dinner, and sleeping
on benches all afternoon, that you've forgotten to ask

5   that truly which thou wouldst truly know. What a devil
hast thou to do with the time of the day? Unless hours
were cups of sack, and minutes capons, and clocks the
tongues of bawds, and dials the signs of leaping-houses,
and the blessed sun himself a fair hot wench in flame-
10   coloured taffeta, I see no reason why thou shouldst be so
superfluous to demand the time of the day.

Falstaff   Indeed, you come near me now, Hal; for we that
take purses go by the moon and the seven stars, and not
by Phoebus, he, that wand'ring knight so fair: and I
15   prithee sweet wag, when thou art king, as God save thy
Grace – Majesty I should say, for grace thou wilt have
none –

Prince   What, none?

Falstaff   No, by my troth, not so much as will serve to be
20   prologue to an egg and butter.

Prince   Well, how then? Come, roundly, roundly.

Falstaff   Marry then sweet wag, when thou art king, let not
us that are the squires of the night's body be called thieves
of the day's beauty: let us be Diana's foresters, gentlemen
25   of the shade, minions of the moon; and let men say we be
men of good government, being governed as the sea is, by
our noble and chaste mistress the moon, under whose
countenance we steal.

Prince   Thou sayest well, and it holds well too, for the
30   fortune of us that are the moon's men doth ebb and flow
like the sea, being governed as the sea is, by the
moon – as for proof now, a purse of gold most resolutely
snatched on Monday night, and most dissolutely spent on
Tuesday morning, got with swearing 'Lay by', and spent
35   with crying 'Bring in', now in as low an ebb as the foot of

what you really want to know. What the devil does it matter to you what time of day it is? Unless hours were glasses of wine, and minutes were chickens, and clocks the tongues of loose women, and dials the signs of brothels, and the sun itself a luscious tart in a red skirt, I see no reason why you should be so irrelevant as to ask the time of day!

Falstaff   You're not far wrong there, Hal! We pickpockets work by moon and starlight – not by [*he sings*] 'Sunshine, my only sunshine!' I beg you, dear boy, when you are King which, God save your Grace – [*he stops, and puts his hand over his mouth in mock shame*] 'Majesty' I should say, not 'Grace' – you'll have no truck with that!

Prince   [*pretending to be shocked*] What? None?

Falstaff   No, upon my life; not even a short one, before a simple snack!

Prince   Well, what then? Come on – [*mocking* **Falstaff's** *circumference with a gesture*] get round to the point!

Falstaff   Well then, dear boy: when you are King, don't let us night-time workers be called daylight-robbers. Let's be moonlight-fingered; stealers through the shadows, followers of the moon. Society should approve of our life-style: like the sea, it's governed by the chaste and noble moon which sheds light on our undertakings!

Prince   Well said! And very apt, too, because we men of the moon have fortunes that ebb and flow like the sea, which is influenced by the moon. For example, on Monday night a purse full of gold is deliberately stolen; on Tuesday morning it is carelessly spent. It's obtained by shouting 'Weapons down'! and spent by saying 'Bottoms up!' One moment it's 'low tide', the bottom

the ladder, and by and by in as high a flow as the ridge of
the gallows.

Falstaff   By the Lord thou say'st true, lad; and is not my
hostess of the tavern a most sweet wench?

40 **Prince**   As the honey of Hybla, my old lad of the castle; and
is not a buff jerkin a most sweet robe of durance?

Falstaff   How now, how now, mad wag? What, in thy
quips and thy quiddities? What a plague have I to do with
a buff jerkin?

45 **Prince**   Why, what a pox have I to do with my hostess of
the tavern?

Falstaff   Well, thou hast called her to a reckoning many a
time and oft.

Prince   Did I ever call for thee to pay thy part?

50 **Falstaff**   No, I'll give thee thy due, thou hast paid all there.

Prince   Yea, and elsewhere, so far as my coin would
stretch, and where it would not I have used my credit.

Falstaff   Yea, and so used it that were it not here apparent
that thou art heir apparent – But I prithee sweet wag,
55 shall there be gallows standing in England when thou art
king? and resolution thus fubbed as it is with the rusty
curb of old father Antic the law? Do not thou when thou
art king hang a thief.

Prince   No, thou shalt.

60 **Falstaff**   Shall I? O rare! By the Lord, I'll be a brave judge.

rung of the gallow's ladder, and the next it's 'high tide' – hanging from the crossbar!

Falstaff   By heaven, that's true, lad. [*Trying to change an unpleasant subject*] But isn't our hostesss here at the tavern a desirable wench?

Prince   A sweet little honey, my lusty old lad! [*Returning to the theme of 'crime doesn't pay'*] However, is a gaolbird's jacket a desirable sort of suit?

Falstaff   [*Realizing the* **Prince** *is rubbing home an unwelcome point*] Now then, now then, you mad jackass! So you're in a funny mood, eh? What the devil have I got to do with a gaolbird's jacket?

Prince   Equally, why subject me to a dose of your tavern hostess?

Falstaff   Well, you've asked for her price-list more than once.

Prince   Did I ever expect you to go shares?

Falstaff   No – I'll give you your due. You settled her account by yourself.

Prince   As always! And as far as my means would stretch! Where it wouldn't, I've used my credit.

Falstaff   Yes – and you've chalked it up so often that were it not 'here apparent' that you are 'heir apparent' . . . [**Falstaff** *stops short, his mind still on the* **Prince's** *earlier uncomfortable theme of crime and punishment*] But tell me, dear boy: when you are King, shall we still have gallows here in England? And will youthful enterprise still be thwarted by that silly old ass, the law? When you are the King, don't hang thieves . . .

Prince   No. You will!

Falstaff   Shall I? Splendid! By God, I'll be an excellent Judge!

Prince   Thou judgest false already. I mean thou shalt have the hanging of the thieves, and so become a rare hangman.

Falstaff   Well, Hal, well; and in some sort it jumps with my humour, as well as waiting in the court, I can tell you.

65 **Prince**   For obtaining of suits?

Falstaff   Yea, for obtaining of suits, whereof the hangman hath no lean wardrobe. 'Sblood, I am as melancholy as a gib-cat, or a lugged bear.

Prince   Or an old lion, or a lover's lute.

70 **Falstaff**   Yea, or the drone of a Lincolnshire bagpipe.

Prince   What sayest thou to a hare, or the melancholy of Moorditch?

Falstaff   Thou hast the most unsavoury similes, and art indeed the most comparative rascalliest sweet young
75 prince. But Hal, I prithee trouble me no more with vanity. I would to God thou and I knew where a commodity of good names were to be bought: an old lord of the Council rated me the other day in the street about you, sir, but I marked him not, and yet he talked very
80 wisely, but I regarded him not, and yet he talked wisely, and in the street too.

Prince   Thou didst well, for wisdom cries out in the streets and no man regards it.

Falstaff   O, thou hast damnable iteration, and art indeed
85 able to corrupt a saint: thou hast done much harm upon me, Hal, God forgive thee for it: before I knew thee, Hal, I knew nothing, and now am I, if a man should speak truly, little better than one of the wicked. I must give over

Prince   You've judged wrongly already. I mean – you'll be in charge of hanging thieves, and become an excellent executioner!

Falstaff   All right, Hal, all right. In a way, it will suit me just as much as waiting around the court, I can tell you.

Prince   To obtain some law suits?

Falstaff   Some suits of clothes, which is the hangman's perk, and the reason why he has a good wardrobe. 'Strewth, I'm as miserable as a tomcat or a baited bear!

Prince   Or an old lion, or a lute played romantically . . .

Falstaff   Yes – or the drone of a Lincolnshire bagpipe . . .

Prince   How about the proverbial melancholy hare, or a miserable place like Moorfields?

Falstaff   You have a gift for finding the most unpleasant likenesses! You're a most comparing, most rascally, sweet young Prince! [*He assumes a solemn and sanctimonious manner*] But Hal, I beg you: trouble me no more with worldly matters. I would to God that you and I knew where we could buy a supply of decent reputations. An elderly Lord of the Council scolded me in public about you, sir: but I took no notice. He talked very wisely, though: but I disregarded him. Yet he did talk sense, and in the street, too . . . .

Prince   You did the right thing. People always ignore wisdom, especially when it's proclaimed in public.

Falstaff   Oh, you've a sinful talent for misquoting holy gospel! You could indeed corrupt a saint! You've done me a lot of harm, Hal, God forgive you for it. Before I knew you, Hal, I was an innocent. Now, to speak the honest truth, I'm little better than one of the wicked. I

90 this life, and I will give it over: by the Lord, and I do not I
am a villain! I'll be damned for never a king's son in
Christendom.

Prince   Where shall we take a purse tomorrow, Jack?

Falstaff   'Zounds, where thou wilt, lad, I'll make one; an I
do not, call me villain and baffle me.

95 **Prince**   I see a good amendment of life in thee, from
praying to purse-taking.

Falstaff   Why, Hal, 'tis my vocation, Hal, 'tis no sin for
a man to labour in his vocation.

[*Enter* **Poins**]

100 Poins! – Now shall we know if Gadshill have set a match.
O, if men were to be saved by merit, what hole in hell
were hot enough for him? This is the most omnipotent
villain that ever cried 'Stand!' to a true man.

Prince   Good morrow, Ned.

105 **Poins**   Good morrow, sweet Hal. What says Monsieur
Remorse? What says Sir John Sack–and–sugar? Jack,
how agrees the devil and thee about thy soul, that thou
soldest him on Good-Friday last, for a cup of Madeira and
a cold capon's leg?

110 **Prince**   Sir John stands to his word, and the devil shall have
his bargain, for he was never yet a breaker of proverbs: he
will give the devil his due.

Poins   Then art thou damned for keeping thy word with
the devil.

must reform. I *shall* reform. By God, if I don't, I'm a villain! I'll not be damned, not for any King's son in Christendom!

Prince   [*mischievously*] Where shall we pinch a purse tomorrow, Jack?

Falstaff   [*himself again*] Hell's bells! Wherever you like, lad! I'm with you! Should I let you down, call me villain and hang me from my heels!

Prince   I see you've been converted – from praying to pick-pocketing!

Falstaff   [*sweetly reasonable*] Why, Hal, it's my calling, Hal. It's no sin for a man to labour at his vocation . . .

[*Enter **Poins***]

[*Greeting him*] Poins! [*To the **Prince***] Now we'll know if Gadshill has planned a robbery. Oh, if men were to be granted salvation for virtuous living, what hole in hell would be sufficiently hot for him? This is the most outrageous villain who ever cried 'Stand and deliver!' to an honest man.

Prince   Good morning, Ned!

Poins   Good morning, dear Hal. What's Mister Remorse saying? What says Sir John Stout-and-Sugar? Jack, how go the negotiations between you and the devil over your soul, which you sold him last Good Friday for a glass of Madeira wine and a cold chicken leg?

Prince   Sir John is keeping to his word. The devil will get his bargain. He was never a man to break a proverb. 'The devil shall have his due'!

Poins   [*to Falstaff*] Then you'll be damned for keeping your word with the devil.

37

Prince   Else he had been damned for cozening the devil.

115 **Poins**   But my lads, my lads, tomorrow morning, by four
o'clock early at Gad's Hill! There are pilgrims going to
Canterbury with rich offerings, and traders riding to
London with fat purses. I have vizards for you all; you
have horses for yourselves. Gadshill lies tonight in
120   Rochester, I have bespoke supper tomorrow night in Eastcheap: we may do it as secure as sleep. If you will go, I
will stuff your purses full of crowns: if you will not, tarry
at home and be hanged.

Falstaff   Hear ye, Yedward: if I tarry at home and go not,
125   I'll hang you for going.

Poins   You will, chops?

Falstaff   Hal, wilt thou make one?

Prince   Who, I rob? I a thief? Not I, by my faith.

Falstaff   There's neither honesty, manhood, nor good
130   fellowship in thee, nor thou cam'st not of the blood royal,
if thou darest not stand for ten shillings.

Prince   Well then, once in my days I'll be a madcap.

Falstaff   Why, that's well said.

Prince   Well, come what will, I'll tarry at home.

135 **Falstaff**   By the Lord, I'll be a traitor then, when thou art
king.

Prince   I care not.

Poins   Sir John, I prithee leave the Prince and me alone: I

Prince   Alternatively, he'll be damned for cheating the devil!

Poins   But my lads, my lads, tomorrow morning, round about four o'clock, there'll be pilgrims passing through Gad's Hill on their way to Canterbury, carrying expensive offerings, and traders riding to London with fat purses. I've got masks for you all, and you've got your own horses. Gadshill is staying overnight at Rochester. I've ordered supper tomorrow night at Eastcheap. We could do it in our sleep. If you'll go, I'll stuff your purses full of crowns. If you won't, stay at home and be hanged to you!

Falstaff   Listen, Ned, if I stay at home and don't go, I'll hang you – for going!

Poins   Will you now, fat chops!

Falstaff   Hal, will you join us?

Prince   [*assuming indignation*] What, me? Be a thief? Not me, that's for sure.

Falstaff   There's neither honesty, manhood, nor comradeship in you, nor are you of royal blood, if you daren't do a job for ten shillings.

Prince   [*pretending to relent under pressure*] All right, then. For once in my life, I'll be a madcap.

Falstaff   Now that's well said.

Prince   [*teasing*] Well, whatever the consequences I'll stay at home.

Falstaff   By God, I'll be a traitor then, when you are King!

Prince   I don't care.

Poins   Sir John, I suggest you leave the Prince and me to

140 will lay him down such reasons for this adventure that he
shall go.

Falstaff   Well, God give thee the spirit of persuasion, and
him the ears of profiting, that what thou speakest may
move, and what he hears may be believed, that the true
prince may (for recreations sake) prove a false thief, for
145 the poor abuses of the time want countenance. Farewell,
you shall find me in Eastcheap.

Prince   Farewell, the latter spring! Farewell, All-hallow
summer!

[*Exit* **Falstaff**]

Poins   Now, my good sweet honey lord, ride with us
150 tomorrow. I have a jest to execute that I cannot manage
alone. Falstaff, Bardolph, Peto, and Gadshill shall rob
those men that we have already waylaid: yourself and I will
not be there: and when they have the booty, if you and I
do not rob them, cut this head off from my shoulders.

155 **Prince**   How shall we part with them in setting forth?

Poins   Why, we will set forth before or after them, and
appoint them a place of meeting, wherein it is at our
pleasure to fail; and then will they adventure upon the
exploit themselves, which they shall have no sooner
160 achieved but we'll set upon them.

Prince   Yea, but 'tis like that they will know us by our
horses, by our habits, and by every other appointment to
be ourselves.

Poins   Tut, our horses they shall not see! I'll tie them in the
165 wood; our vizards we will change after we leave them; and
sirrah, I have cases of buckram for the nonce, to immask
our noted outward garments.

ourselves. I'll give him such good reasons for this adventure that he'll go.

Falstaff [*piously*] Well, God inspire you with the gift of persuasion, and him the capacity to learn from it, so that what you speak may influence, and what he hears may be believed. Then the true prince may, for the fun of it, prove to be a false thief. It's time royalty took notice of the maladies of our times. Farewell: you'll find me in Eastcheap!

Prince Farewell, late Spring! Farewell, Indian Summer!

[**Falstaff** *leaves*]

Poins Now, my good, sweet honey-lord, join the ride tomorrow. I've planned a practical joke that I can't manage alone. Falstaff, Bardolph, Peto, and Gadshill will rob the men we've set our trap for, but you and I will not be there. When they've got the booty, if you and I don't then rob them – chop my head from off my shoulders!

Prince How can we separate ourselves from them at the outset?

Poins Why, we'll start before or after them, and agree a meeting-place. Then we won't turn up. They'll proceed on their own, and as soon as they've done the job, we'll set upon them.

Prince Yes, but they'll recognize us by our horses, our clothes, and by the rest of our equipment . . .

Poins No, they won't see our horses. I'll tether them in the wood. We'll change our masks after we leave them. And I have rough buckram suits ready for the occasion, to cover our well-known clothes.

Prince   Yea, but I doubt they will be too hard for us.

Poins   Well, for two of them, I know them to be as true-
170   bred cowards as ever turned back; and for the third, if he
fight longer than he sees reason, I'll forswear arms. The
virtue of this jest will be the incomprehensible lies that
this same fat rogue will tell us when we meet at supper,
how thirty at least he fought with, what wards, what
175   blows, what extremities he endured; and in the reproof of
this lives the jest.

Prince   Well, I'll go with thee. Provide us all things
necessary, and meet me tomorrow night in Eastcheap;
there I'll sup. Farewell.

180   **Poins**   Farewell, my lord.

Prince   I know you all, and will awhile uphold
The unyoked humour of your idleness.
Yet herein will I imitate the sun,
Who doth permit the base contagious clouds
185   To smother up his beauty from the world,
That, when he please again to be himself,
Being wanted he may be more wondered at
By breaking through the foul and ugly mists
Of vapours that did seem to strangle him.
190   If all the year were playing holidays,
To sport would be as tedious as to work;
But when they seldom come, they wished-for come,
And nothing pleaseth but rare accidents:
So when this loose behaviour I throw off,
195   And pay the debt I never promised,
By how much better than my word I am,
By so much shall I falsify men's hopes;
And like bright metal on a sullen ground,
My reformation, glitt'ring o'er my fault,
200   Shall show more goodly, and attract more eyes

Prince   Yes, but I'm afraid they'll be too tough for us.

Poins   Well, as for two of them, I know they are as thorough going cowards as ever ran away. As for the third [*meaning* **Falstaff**] if he fights a moment longer than he sees sense in it, I'll give up wearing a sword. The great joy of this joke will be in the outrageous lies this fat rogue will tell us when we meet at supper. How he fought with thirty men at least . . . his defensive strokes . . . the blows he took . . . the tight corners he was in. The fun will be in revealing the true facts!

Prince   Well, I'll go along with you. Get all the necessaries together, and join me at Eastcheap tomorrow night. I'll dine there. Adieu!

Poins   Adieu, my lord!

[*He goes*]

Prince   I know you all for what you are. For the present, I'll go along with your rowdy misbehaviour and your worthlessness. This way, I'll copy the sun. He allows the dark, unhealthy clouds to conceal his beauty from the world, so that when it suits him to be seen again, having been missed, he's all the more admired for breaking through the foul and ugly mists that seemed to have him stifled. If all-year-round were one long holiday, to play would be as tedious as to work. But when holidays are few and far between, we look forward to them. Nothing is more pleasant than occasional events. So when I abandon this loose living, and redeem myself (although I never promised to), the more I prove my life-style is reformed, the greater shall I show I've been misjudged. And like bright metal on a dull background, my reformation – outshining all my faults – will look more impressive, and attract more attention, than conduct

Than that which hath no foil to set it off.
I'll so offend, to make offence a skill,
Redeeming time when men think least I will.

[*Exit*]

Scene 3

Windsor. The Council Chamber. Enter the **King,
Northumberland, Worcester, Hotspur, Sir Walter
Blunt,** *with others.*

King   My blood hath been too cold and temperate,
      Unapt to stir at these indignities,
      And you have found me, for accordingly
      You tread upon my patience; but be sure
5   I will from henceforth rather be myself,
      Mighty, and to be feared, than my condition,
      Which hath been smooth as oil, soft as young down,
      And therefore lost that title of respect
      Which the proud soul ne'er pays but to the proud.

10 **Worcester**   Our house, my sovereign liege, little deserves
      The scourge of greatness to be used on it,
      And that same greatness too which our own hands
      Have help to make so portly.

   Northumberland   My lord –

15 **King**   Worcester, get thee gone, for I do see
      Danger and disobedience in thine eye:
      O sir, your presence is too bold and peremptory,
      And majesty might never yet endure

that has never been amiss. I'll offend in such a way as to turn offence into an art, changing my ways when the world least expects me to.

[*He goes*]

Scene 3

The Council Chamber at Windsor Castle. Enter the **King,**
Northumberland, Worcester, Hotspur, Sir Walter Blunt, *and*
others. The **King,** *having been crossed by* **Worcester,** *is*
angry.

King   I've been too cool and mild-mannered – disinclined to react against indignities – and you have detected this, and tried my patience accordingly. But I can assure you that henceforth I will respond like a King, mighty and to be feared, rather than follow my natural disposition: which is to be easy-going and gentle, losing me the respect to which I'm entitled, and which is only given by those in authority to men of authority.

Worcester   The House of Worcester, my sovereign liege, little deserves to be scourged by the great; especially when we have helped with our own hands to give that greatness so much dignity . . .

Northumberland   My lord –

King   [*interrupting and pointing to the door*] Worcester, be off with you! I can see danger and disobedience in your looks. Yes, sir: your manner is too bold and familiar. No king can tolerate a subject's angry and defiant frown.

45

The moody frontier of a servant brow.
You have good leave to leave us: when we need
20 Your use and counsel we shall send for you.

[*Exit* **Worcester**]

You were about to speak.

Northumberland   Yea, my good lord.
Those prisoners in your Highness' name demanded,
25 Which Harry Percy here at Holmedon took,
Were, as he says, not with such strength denied
As is delivered to your Majesty.
Either envy therefore, or misprision,
Is guilty of this fault, and not my son.

Hotspur   My liege, I did deny no prisoners,
But I remember, when the fight was done,
30 When I was dry with rage, and extreme toil,
Breathless and faint, leaning upon my sword,
Came there a certain lord, neat and trimly dressed,
Fresh as a bridegroom, and his chin new reaped
Showed like a stubble land at harvest home.
35 He was perfumed like a milliner,
And 'twixt his finger and his thumb he held
A pouncet-box, which ever and anon
He gave his nose, and took't away again –
Who therewith angry, when it next came there,
40 Took it in snuff; and still he smiled and talked:
And as the soldiers bore dead bodies by,
He called them untaught knaves, unmannerly,
To bring a slovenly unhandsome corse
Betwixt the wind and his nobility.
45 With many holiday and lady terms
He questioned me, amongst the rest demanded
My prisoners in your Majesty's behalf.
I then, all smarting with my wounds being cold,

You have our full permission to leave us. When we need
your services and your advice, we'll send for you!

[**Worcester** *suppresses a reply and leaves*]

[*To* **Northumberland**] You were about to speak?

Northumberland   Yes, my good lord. Those prisoners which
Harry Percy took at Holmedon, and which were
demanded in your Highness's name, were not, as he
says, denied with such vigour as was reported to your
Majesty. Either malice or a genuine mistake is guilty of
this fault, not my son.

Hotspur   My liege, I denied you no prisoners. But I do
remember, after the battle was over, when I
was exhausted with frustration and extreme effort,
breathless and faint, leaning on my sword, a certain
lord turned up, neat and trimly dressed, fresh as a
bridegroom, and his chin, recently clipped, looked like a
field of stubble at harvest-time. He was perfumed like a
hat-maker, and between his finger and his thumb he held
a scent bottle, which every now and then he put to his
nose, then took it away again: at which his nose got
angry, and sniffed its disapproval, when he next
presented it. And still he went on smiling and talking;
and as the soldiers carried the dead bodies away, he
called them 'ignorant knaves', 'unmannerly', to bring a
nasty, ugly corpse between his noble self and the wind.
With many posh and pansy words he chatted at me, and
amongst the rest, demanded my prisoners on your
Majesty's behalf. All smarting as I was with my wounds

To be so pestered with a popinjay,
50 Out of my grief and my impatience
Answered neglectingly, I know not what,
He should, or he should not, for he made me mad
To see him shine so brisk, and smell so sweet,
And talk so like a waiting-gentlewoman
55 Of guns, and drums, and wounds, God save the mark!
And telling me the sovereignest thing on earth
Was parmacity for an inward bruise,
And that it was great pity, so it was,
This villainous saltpetre should be digged
60 Out of the bowels of the harmless earth,
Which many a good tall fellow had destroyed
So cowardly, and but for these vile guns
He would himself have been a soldier.
This bald unjointed chat of his, my lord,
65 I answered indirectly, as I said,
And I beseech you, let not his report
Come current for an accusation
Betwixt my love and your high Majesty.

Blunt   The circumstances considered, good my lord,
70 Whate'er Lord Harry Percy then had said
To such a person, and in such a place,
At such a time, with all the rest retold,
May reasonably die, and never rise
To do him wrong, or any way impeach
75 What then he said, so he unsay it now.

King   Why, yet he doth deny his prisoners,
But with proviso and exception,
That we at our own charge shall ransom straight
His brother-in-law, the foolish Mortimer,
80 Who, on my soul, hath wilfully betrayed
The lives of those that he did lead to fight
Against that great magician, damned Glendower,

congealing, and being so pestered with a gaudy parrot, I
answered off-handedly because of my pain and my short-
temper. Exactly what I said I do not know: whether he
could have them, or he couldn't. He made me furious to
see him look so smart, and smell so sweet, and hear him
talk just like a lady's maid of guns, and drums, and
wounds – God help us! – and telling me 'the most super
thing on earth' for an internal bruise was spermaceti
ointment; and that it was 'a great pity, it really was', that
this 'wretched gunpowder' should be dug from the
bowels of the harmless earth, which many a stalwart
man had so cowardly destroyed; and but for these 'vile
guns' he would have been a soldier himself. . . . This
empty, rambling chat of his, my lord, I answered
casually, as I said, and I beg you not to let his report be
taken at face value, as an accusation standing between
my loyalty and your high Majesty.

Blunt   [*to the* **King**] Considering the circumstances, good
my lord, whatever Lord Harry Percy then said at that time
to such a person, and in such a place, at such a time,
with everything else as described: it should all be
forgotten, never to be held against him, or cited as
disloyal provided he retracts it now.

King   But he still witholds his prisoners, with the one
proviso and condition: that at our own expense, we
should immediately pay the ransom for his brother-in-
law, the foolish Mortimer. But, upon my soul, Mortimer
wilfully betrayed the lives of those he led to fight against
that great magician, damned Glendower, the one whose

Whose daughter, as we hear, the Earl of March
Hath lately married. Shall our coffers then
85   Be emptied to redeem a traitor home?
Shall we buy treason, and indent with fears
When they have lost and forfeited themselves?
No, on the barren mountains let him starve;
For I shall never hold that man my friend
90   Whose tongue shall ask me for one penny cost
To ransom home revolted Mortimer.

Hotspur   Revolted Mortimer?
He never did fall off, my sovereign liege,
But by the chance of war: to prove that true
95   Needs no more but one tongue for all those wounds,
Those mouthed wounds, which valiantly he took,
When on the gentle Severn's sedgy bank,
In single opposition hand to hand,
He did confound the best part of an hour
100   In changing hardiment with great Glendower.
Three times they breathed, and three times did they drink
Upon agreement of swift Severn's flood,
Who then affrighted with their bloody looks
Ran fearfully among the trembling reeds,
105   And hid his crisp head in the hollow bank,
Bloodstained with these valiant combatants.
Never did bare and rotten policy
Colour her working with such deadly wounds,
Nor never could the noble Mortimer
110   Receive so many, and all willingly:
Then let not him be slandered with revolt.

King   Thou dost belie him, Percy, thou dost belie him,
He never did encounter with Glendower:
I tell thee, he durst as well have met the devil alone
115   As Owen Glendower for an enemy.
Art thou not ashamed? But sirrah, henceforth

daughter, so we hear, was recently married to the Earl of
March. Shall we pay for treason, subsidise cowards,
when they themselves surrendered? No. He can starve
on the bare mountains. I'll never call a man my friend
who voices a request for so much as a penny to ransom
home traitorous Mortimer!

Hotspur   The traitorous Mortimer? He never let you down,
my sovereign liege, except through the fortunes of war.
To prove the truth of that, only one tongue need speak
for all those wounds, those mouthlike wounds, which he
so valiantly suffered, when he spent the best part of an
hour exchanging blows with the great Glendower, in
single combat, hand to hand, on the grassy banks of the
gentle River Severn. Three times they paused for breath,
and three times they drank by agreement from the fast
moving Severn, which, terrified by their bloody looks, ran
frightened among the trembling reeds, hiding its rippled
surface, and pressing against the hollow bank, stained
with the blood of these valiant combatants. Never did
barefaced cunning hide behind such deadly wounds, nor
could the noble Mortimer receive so many, and all
willingly. So don't let him be slandered with *treason*!

King   You misrepresent him, Percy – you misrepresent him!
He never fought with Owen Glendower! I tell you, he
might as well have met the devil on his own, as
Glendower for an enemy. Are you not ashamed? Be that

51

Let me not hear you speak of Mortimer:
Send me your prisoners with the speediest means,
Or you shall hear in such a kind from me
120   As will displease you. My Lord Nothumberland:
We license your departure with your son.
Send us your prisoners, or you will hear of it.

[*Exit* **King**, *with* **Blunt** *and train*]

Hotspur   And if the devil come and roar for them
I will not send them. I will after straight
125   And tell him so, for I will ease my heart,
Albeit I make a hazard of my head.

Northumberland   What, drunk with choler? Stay, and
pause awhile,
Here comes your uncle.

[*Enter* **Worcester**]

Hotspur   Speak of Mortimer?
'Zounds, I will speak of him, and let my soul
130   Want mercy if I do not join with him!
Yea, on his part I'll empty all these veins,
And shed my dear blood, drop by drop in the dust,
But I will lift the down-trod Mortimer
As high in the air as this unthankful King,
135   As this ingrate and cankered Bolingbroke.

Northumberland   Brother, the King hath made your
nephew mad.

Worcester   Who struck this heat up after I was gone?

Hotspur   He will forsooth have all my prisoners,
And when I urged the ransom once again
140   Of my wife's brother, then his cheek looked pale,

as it may, sir: in future, don't let me hear you mention Mortimer. Send me your prisoners by the quickest means, or you shall hear from me in a way that you won't like! My Lord Northumberland: you may go now with your son. [*To* **Hotspur**] Send us your prisoners, or you will hear of it!

[*The* **King** *exits angrily, followed by* **Blunt** *and the Court officials*]

Hotspur   [*enraged*] Even if the devil himself comes and roars for them, I won't send them! I'll go after him immediately and tell him so. It will make me feel better, although I might be risking my head!

Northumberland   [*rebuking him*] What, drunk with anger? Stay where you are, and cool down. Here comes your uncle.

[**Worcester** *returns*]

Hotspur   [*fuming still*] Speak of Mortimer? By God, I'll speak of him – and may my soul lack mercy if I don't ally with him. Yes, in his cause I'll drain my very veins, shed my precious blood drop by drop in the dust but I'll lift the down-trodden Mortimer as high in the air as this unthankful King – as this ungrateful and rotten-hearted Bolingbroke!

Northumberland   [*to* **Worcester**] Brother, the King has made your nephew mad.

Worcester   Who started the argument after I left?

Hotspur   He'll have all my prisoners, no less! And when I repeated my plea for the ransom of my wife's brother, he

And on my face he turned an eye of death,
Trembling even at the name of Mortimer.

Worcester   I cannot blame him: was not he proclaimed,
By Richard that dead is, the next of blood?

145 **Northumberland**   He was, I heard the proclamation:
And then it was, when the unhappy King
(Whose wrongs in us God pardon!) did set forth
Upon his Irish expedition;
From whence he, intercepted, did return
150 To be deposed, and shortly murdered.

Worcester   And for whose death we in the world's wide
mouth
Live scandalized and foully spoken of.

Hotspur   But soft, I pray you, did King Richard then
Proclaim my brother Edmund Mortimer
155 Heir to the crown?

Northumberland   He did, myself did hear it.

Hotspur   Nay, then I cannot blame his cousin King,
That wished him on the barren mountains starve.
But shall it be that you that set the crown
Upon the head of this forgetful man,
160 And for his sake wear the detested blot
Of murderous subornation – shall it be
That you a world of curses undergo,
Being the agents, or base second means,
The cords, the ladder, or the hangman rather?
165 – O, pardon me, that I descend so low,
To show the line and the predicament
Wherein you range under this subtle King!
Shall it for shame be spoken in these days,
Or fill up chronicles in time to come,
170 That men of your nobility and power

went white, and gave me a look that could kill, trembling at the very name of Mortimer!

Worcester   I can't blame him. Wasn't he named by the late King Richard as the next in line?

Northumberland   He was: I heard the proclamation. And it was then that the unhappy King – God pardon us for wronging him! – set out on his Irish expedition, from which he broke off to return, be deposed, and quickly murdered.

Worcester   And for whose death we are scandalized and denigrated by the whole wide world.

Hotspur   But just a moment, now . . . . Did King Richard actually proclaim my brother-in-law Edmund Mortimer the heir to the crown?

Northumberland   He did, I heard it myself.

Hotspur   Well then, I can't blame his cousin the King for wanting him to starve to death on a barren mountain. Can you – that set the crown upon the head of this forgetful man, and for whose sake you carry the stigma of aiding and abetting murder – can you really endure the burden of universal abuse for being his agents: the contemptible henchmen, the ropes, the ladder, the hangmen even? Pardon my stooping so low as to rank you in descending order below this subtle King! Shall it be shamefully said today, or be written down in the history books of tomorrow, that men of your nobility and

Didgage them both in an unjust behalf
(As both of you, God pardon it, have done)
To put down Richard, that sweet lovely rose,
And plant this thorn, this canker Bolingbroke?
175 And shall it in more shame be further spoken,
That you are fooled, discarded, and shook off
By him for whom these shames ye underwent?
No, yet time serves wherein you may redeem
Your banished honours, and restore yourselves
180 Into the good thoughts of the world again:
Revenge the jeering and disdained contempt
Of this proud King, who studies day and night
To answer all the debt he owes to you,
Even with the bloody payment of your deaths:
185 Therefore, I say –

Worcester   Peace, cousin, say no more.
And now I will unclasp a secret book,
And to your quick-conceiving discontents
I'll read you matter deep and dangerous,
190 As full of peril and adventurous spirit
As to o'er-walk a current roaring loud
On the unsteadfast footing of a spear.

Hotspur   If he fall in, good night, or sink, or swim!
Send danger from the east unto the west,
So honour cross it from the north to south,
195 And let them grapple: O, the blood more stirs
To rouse a lion than to start a hare!

Northumberland   Imagination of some great exploit
Drives him beyond the bounds of patience.

Hotspur   By heaven, methinks it were an easy leap
200 To pluck bright honour from the pale-faced moon,
Or dive into the bottom of the deep,
Where fathom-line could never touch the ground,

power actually supported injustice (as both of you, God forgive you, have done) to topple Richard – that sweet, lovely rose – in order to plant this thorn, this cancerous growth, Bolingbroke? And shall it be even more shamefully said, that you are fooled, discarded, and shaken off by the very man on whose behalf you undertook these shameful deeds? No. But there is still time for you to redeem your banished honours, and to restore your good names in the world's reckoning. Revenge the jeers and the disdainful contempt of this haughty King, who schemes by day and night to settle his debts to you, the payment being your violent deaths! Therefore, I say –

Worcester   Sh, cousin! Say no more. Now I'll let you into a secret, appealing to that sharp sense of grievance of yours. I'll tell you of a deep and dangerous scheme: as full of risk and hazard as stepping over sword edges to cross a stream . . .

Hotspur   If a man falls in, it's farewell to him whether he sinks or swims! In pursuing a path of honour, it little matters if danger crosses it. It takes more to rouse a lion than to frighten a hare!

Northumberland   [*To* **Worcester**] Thoughts of heroic enterprises turn his head . . .

Hotspur   By heavens, I don't think there's any problem in snatching shining Honour from the pale-faced moon, or diving to the bottom of the sea, where fathom lines can

And pluck up drowned honour by the locks,
So he that doth redeem her thence might wear
205 Without corrival all her dignities:
But out upon this half-faced fellowship!

Worcester   He apprehends a world of figures here,
But not the form of what he should attend:
Good cousin, give me audience for a while.

210 **Hotspur**   I cry you mercy.

Worcester   Those same noble Scots
That are your prisoners –

Hotspur   I'll keep them all!
By God he shall not have a Scot of them,
No, if a Scot would save his soul he shall not.
I'll keep them, by this hand!

Worcester   You start away,
215 And lend no ear unto my purposes:
Those prisoners you shall keep.

Hotspur   Nay, I will! That's flat!
He said he would not ransom Mortimer,
Forbade my tongue to speak of Mortimer,
220 But I will find him when he lies asleep,
And in his ear I'll holla 'Mortimer!',
Nay, I'll have a starling shall be taught to speak
Nothing but 'Mortimer', and give it him
To keep his anger still in motion.

Worcester   Hear you, cousin, a word.

225 **Hotspur**   All studies here I solemnly defy,
Save how to gall and pinch this Bolingbroke:
And that same sword-and-buckler Prince of Wales,
But that I think his father loves him not,
And would be glad he met with some mischance –
230 I would have him poisoned with a pot of ale!

never reach, to pull up drowning Honour by the hair!
But the rescuer must get all the credit: none of this
half-baked sharing!

Worcester   [*To* **Northumberland**] He is in a world of his
own imagination here – he's not dealing with realities.
[*To* **Hotspur**] Nephew dear, listen to me a moment . . .

Hotspur   [*calming down*] My apologies . . .

Worcester   Those noble Scots who are your prisoners –

Hotspur   [*furious again*] I'll keep them all! By God, he'll not
have a single Scot of them! Not if they were offered
Scot-free to save his soul, he won't! I'll keep them, I
swear I will!

Worcester   Off you go, ignoring what I say to you! Those
prisoners you shall keep . . .

Hotspur   No – I will! That's flat! He said he wouldn't
ransom Mortimer! Forbade me to speak of Mortimer! But
I'll catch him when he's fast asleep, and I'll shout
'Mortimer!' into his ear. What's more, I'll have a parrot
taught to say nothing but 'Mortimer', and give it to him
to keep his anger on the go.

Worcester   If I can say something, nephew –

Hotspur   [*ignoring his uncle*] I solemnly renounce all
occupations excepting one: how to annoy and irritate
this Bolingbroke! And as for that tinpot Prince of Wales,
if it wasn't for the fact that I think his father dislikes him,
and would be glad if he came to some harm, I'd have him
poisoned with a pot of ale!

Worcester   Farewell, kinsman: I'll talk to you
When you are better tempered to attend.

Northumberland   Why, what a wasp-stung and impatient
fool
Art thou to break into this woman's mood,
235   Tying thine ear to no tongue but thine own!

Hotspur   Why, look you, I am whipped and scourged with
rods,
Nettled, and stung with pismires, when I hear
Of this vile politician Bolingbroke.
In Richard's time – what do you call the place?
240   A plague upon it! It is in Gloucestershire –
'Twas where the mad-cap Duke his uncle kept,
His uncle York – where I first bowed my knee
Unto this king of smiles, this Bolingbroke,
'Sblood, when you and he came back from Ravenspurgh –

245 **Northumberland**   At Berkeley Castle.

Hotspur   You say true.
Why, what a candy deal of courtesy
This fawning greyhound then did proffer me!
'Look when his infant fortune came to age',
And 'gentle Harry Percy', and 'kind cousin':
250   O, the devil take such cozeners! – God forgive me!
Good uncle, tell your tale; I have done.

Worcester   Nay, if you have not, to it again,
We will stay your leisure.

Hotspur   I have done, i'faith.

255 **Worcester**   Then once more to your Scottish prisoners;
Deliver them up without their ransom straight,
And make the Douglas' son your only mean
For powers in Scotland, which, for divers reasons
Which I shall send you written, be assured

Worcester   [*giving up*] Farewell, kinsman. I'll talk to you when you are in a better mood for listening.

Northumberland   Why, what a waspish and impatient fool you are to break into this shrewish mood, hearing nothing but the sound of your own voice!

Hotspur   Why, don't you see, I'm whipped and scourged with rods, stung by ants and nettles, whenever I hear of this vile schemer Bolingbroke. In Richard's day – what do you call the place? Damn it, it's in Gloucestershire – it was where the reckless Duke's uncle lived – his uncle the Duke of York – where I first bowed at the knees before this king of smiles, this Bolingbroke – God! – when you and he came back from Ravenspurgh –

Northumberland   [*patiently*] At Berkeley Castle.

Hotspur   That's right. Why, what a sugar-stick of politeness this fawning greyhound offered me then! 'Infant promise realized!', and 'Gentle Harry Percy', and 'Kind cousin'! Oh, the devil take such tricksters! [*He remembers he is doing it again*] God forgive me! Good uncle, speak your story. I've finished.

Worcester   [*wrily*] Well, if you haven't, off you go again. We'll await your pleasure.

Hotspur   [*subdued*] I've finished, honestly.

Worcester   Then to return to your Scottish prisoners. Deliver them up straight away without their ransoms, and make Douglas's son your single surety for a Scottish army which, for various reasons which I'll put in writing,

Will easily be granted – (*To* **Northumberland**) You, my
lord,
260 Your son in Scotland being thus employed,
Shall secretly into the bosom creep
Of that same noble prelate well-beloved,
The Archbishop.

Hotspur   Of York, is it not?

Worcester   True, who bears
hard
His brother's death at Bristow, the Lord Scroop.
265 I speak not this in estimation,
As what I think might be, but what I know
Is ruminated, plotted, and set down,
And only stays but to behold the face
Of that occasion that shall bring it on.

270 **Hotspur**   I smell it. Upon my life it will do well!

Northumberland   Before the game is afoot thou still let'st
slip.

Hotspur   Why, it cannot choose but be a noble plot;
And then the power of Scotland, and of York,
To join with Mortimer, ha?

Worcester   And so they shall.

275 **Hotspur**   In faith it is exceedingly well aimed.

Worcester   And 'tis no little reason bids us speed,
To save our heads by raising of a head;
For, bear ourselves as even as we can,
The King will always think him in our debt,
280 And think we think ourselves unsatisfied,
Till he hath found a time to pay us home:
And see already how he doth begin
To make us strangers to his looks of love.

you can be certain will easily be granted. [*to*
Northumberland] Meanwhile you, my lord, while your
son is thus employed in Scotland, shall secretly connive
with that noble and well-beloved churchman, the
Archbishop.

Hotspur   Of York, you mean?

Worcester   Indeed. He has a grievance over his brother's
execution at Bristol, the Lord Scroop. This is no guesswork, or what I think might be, but what I know, is
discussed, plotted, and set down. All it waits for is the
right opportunity.

Hotspur   I get the point. Upon my soul, that's very good!

Northumberland   Before we've even begun, you're past the
starting-post!

Hotspur   Why, it can't be anything less than an excellent
plot! Then the armies of Scotland and York will join with
Mortimer, eh?

Worcester   That's the idea.

Hotspur   Really, it's exceedingly well planned.

Worcester   And there's good reason to act quickly: saving
our heads by taking up arms. Because however much we
try not to be troublesome, the King will always think he's
in our debt, and believe we are dissatisfied, until such
time as he can pay us out. See how already he's beginning to deny us his cordial looks.

Hotspur   He does, he does! We'll be revenged on him.

285 **Worcester**   Cousin, farewell. No further go in this
Than I by letters shall direct your course.
When time is ripe, which will be suddenly,
I'll steal to Glendower, and Lord Mortimer,
Where you, and Douglas, and our powers at once,
290 As I will fashion it, shall happily meet,
To bear our fortunes in our own strong arms,
Which now we hold at much uncertainty.

Northumberland   Farewell, good brother. We shall thrive,
I trust.

295 **Hotspur**   Uncle, adieu: O, let the hours be short,
Till fields, and blows, and groans applaud our sport!

[*Exeunt*]

Hotspur   He does! He does! We'll be revenged on him!

Worcester   Nephew, goodbye. Don't take any action other than what's advised in my letters. When the time's ripe, which will be soon, I'll go secretly to Glendower and Lord Mortimer. There you, Douglas and our armies will conveniently assemble, as I'll arrange. Then we can look after our interests from a position of strength: right now we are in danger.

Northumberland   Farewell, good brother. We shall prosper, I trust.

Hotspur   Uncle, adieu. May time fly till battlefields, and blows, and groans are all our game!

Act two

Scene 1

Rochester. An Inn Yard. Enter a **Carrier** *with a lantern in his hand.*

First Carrier   Heigh-ho! An it be not four by the day I'll be hanged; Charles' wain is over the new chimney, and yet our horse not packed. What, ostler!

Ostler   [*Within*] Anon, anon.

5 **First Carrier**   I prithee, Tom, beat Cut's saddle, put a few flocks in the point; poor jade is wrung in the withers out of all cess.

[*Enter another* **Carrier**]

Second Carrier   Peas and beans are as dank here as a dog, and that is the next way to give poor jades the bots. This
10   house is turned upside down since Robin Ostler died.

First Carrier   Poor fellow never joyed since the price of oats rose, it was the death of him.

Second Carrier   I think this be the most villainous house in all London road for fleas, I am stung like a tench.

15 **First Carrier**   Like a tench! By the mass, there is ne'er a king christen could be better bit than I have been since the first cock.

Second Carrier   Why, they will allow us ne'er a jordan, and then we leak in your chimney, and your chamber-lye
20   breeds fleas like a loach.

Act two

Scene 1

An inn yard at Rochester. Enter a **Porter**, *with a lantern in his hand*

1st Porter [*yawning*] Heigh ho! I'll be hanged if it ain't four o'clock in the morning. [*Looking up at the sky*] The Plough's up higher than the new chimney and our horses are still not loaded up. Hey, Groom!

Groom [*inside*] Coming, coming!

1st Porter 'Ere, Tom: give Cut's saddle a good thumping to soften it up, and stuff some padding into the pommel. The poor animal is proper raw round the shoulders.

[*Enter a second* **Porter**]

2nd Porter The peas and beans here are as damp as a wet dog. That's the quickest way to give these poor creatures the worms. This house is turned upside down since Robin Ostler died.

1st Porter The poor fellow never had much joy after the price of oats rose. It was the death of him.

2nd Porter [*scratching*] I think this must be the most villainous house in all London Road for fleas. I've got as many red spots as a tench.

1st Porter As a tench! Dammit, there's never a Christian king been better bit than I have, since midnight!

2nd Porter Well, they won't give us chamber-pots, so we pee in the chimney: and piss breeds fleas like a loach.

First Carrier   What, ostler! Come away, and be hanged, come away!

Second Carrier   I have a gammon of bacon, and two razes of ginger, to be delivered as far as Charing Cross.

25 **First Carrier**   God's body! The turkeys in my pannier are quite starved. What, ostler! A plague on thee, hast thou never an eye in thy head? canst not hear? And 'twere not as good deed as drink to break the pate on thee, I am a very villain. Come, and be hanged! Hast no faith in thee?

[*Enter* **Gadshill**]

30 **Gadshill**   Good morrow, carriers, what's o'clock?

First Carrier   I think it be two o'clock.

Gadshill   I prithee lend me thy lantern, to see my gelding in the stable.

First Carrier   Nay, by God, soft! I know a trick worth two 35 of that, i'faith.

Gadshill   I pray thee lend me thine.

Second Carrier   Ay, when? Canst tell? Lend me thy lantern, quoth he! Marry I'll see thee hanged first.

Gadshill   Sirrah carrier, what time do you mean to come to 40 London?

Second Carrier   Time enough to go to bed with a candle, I warrant thee; come, neighbour Mugs, we'll call up the gentlemen, they will along with company, for they have great charge.

[*Exeunt* **Carriers**]

1st Porter   Hey, Groom! Come along here, and be hanged!
Come along!

2nd Porter   I've got a haunch of bacon and two ginger
roots to deliver as far as Charing Cross.

1st Porter   God almighty! The turkeys in my basket are
starving. Hey, Groom! Blast you, haven't you got no
eyes? Can't you hear? I'm a villain if it wouldn't do you
the world of good to have your head bashed. Come
along, and be hanged to you! Have you no sense of
service?

[*Enter* **Gadshill**]

Gadshill   'Morning, Carriers. What's the time?

1st Porter   I think it's two o'clock.

Gadshill   Lend me your lantern, will you, to see my gelding
in the stable.

1st Porter   Nay, by God! Listen to him! I know a trick worth
two of that, indeed!

Gadshill   [*to* **2nd Porter**] Please – lend me yours.

2nd Porter   Time enough to light candles at bed-time, I can
tell you! [*To* **1st Porter**] Come on, Neighbour Mugs, we'll
rouse the gentlemen. They'll want travelling companions,
'cos they've got plenty of luggage to look after.

[*The* **Porters** *depart*]

45 **Gadshill**   What ho! Chamberlain!

[*Enter* **Chamberlain**]

Chamberlain   'At hand, quoth pick-purse.'

Gadshill   That's even as fair as 'At hand, quoth the
chamberlain': for thou variest no more from picking of
purses than giving direction doth from labouring; thou
50   layest the plot how.

Chamberlain   Good morrow, master Gadshill. It holds
current that I told you yesternight: there's a franklin in the
Wild of Kent hath brought three hundred marks with him
in gold, I heard him tell it to one of his company last
55   night at supper, a kind of auditor, one that hath abun-
dance of charge too, God knows what; they are up already,
and call for eggs and butter. They will away presently.

Gadshill   Sirrah, if they meet not with Saint Nicholas'
clerks, I'll give thee this neck.

60 **Chamberlain**   No, I'll none of it, I pray thee keep that for
the hangman, for I know thou worshippest Saint Nicholas,
as truly as a man of falsehood may.

Gadshill   What talkest thou to me of the hangman? If I
hang, I'll make a fat pair of gallows: for if I hang, old Sir
65   John hangs with me, and thou knowest he is no starveling.
Tut, there are other Troyans that thou dream'st not of,
the which for sport sake are content to do the profession
some grace, that would (if matters should be looked into)
for their own credit sake make all whole. I am joined with
70   no foot-landrakers, no long-staff sixpenny strikers, none of
these mad mustachio purple-hued maltworms, but with
nobility and tranquillity, burgomasters and great onyers,
such as can hold in, such as will strike sooner than speak,

Gadshill   Hey there! Chamberlain!

[*The* **Chamberlain** *enters*]

Chamberlain   'Here at hand – said the pick-pocket!'

Gadshill   That's about the same as saying 'Here at hand said the chamberlain'. You are about as far removed from picking pockets as bossing is from labouring. You do all the planning.

Chamberlain   'Morning Mister Gadshill. What I told you last night is right. There's a wealthy farmer from the Kent area with £200 on him in gold. I heard him tell one of his companions so, last night at supper: a kind of Revenue Officer, who's also loaded, too, with God-knows-what. They're up already, calling for scrambled eggs. They want to be off immediately.

Gadshill   If they don't meet with highwaymen, you can have my neck!

Chamberlain   No, thanks – keep it for the hangman! I know you worship their patron St Nicholas as devotedly as any faithless man can!

Gadshill   Why talk to me about hangmen? If I ever hang, I'll make a fat pair on the gallows: 'cos if I hang, old Sir John hangs with me, and he's no skeleton as you know! Why, there are others in our gang that you'd never dream belonged to it: who for the fun of it are glad to give the profession some class. If ever any questions were asked, they'd see us in the clear for their own reputations' sake. I don't mix with your homeless sneak-thieves, or your paltry cheapskate pick-pockets, your purple-faced, bewhiskered beer swillers; only with the nobility and the gentry, Lord Mayors and great Somebodies – the type that rally round together, and who'd as soon cosh as

71

75 and speak sooner than drink, and drink sooner than
pray – and yet, 'zounds, I lie, for they pray continually to
their saint the commonwealth, or rather not pray to her,
but prey on her, for they ride up and down on her, and
make her their boots.

Chamberlain   What, the commonwealth their boots? will
80 she hold out water in foul way?

Gadshill   She will, she will, justice hath liquored her: we
steal as in a castle, cock-sure: we have the receipt of fern-
seed, we walk invisible.

Chamberlain   Nay, by my faith, I think you are more
85 beholding to the night than to fern-seed for your walking
invisible.

Gadshill   Give me thy hand, thou shalt have a share in our
purchase, as I am a true man.

Chamberlain   Nay, rather let me have it, as you are a false
90 thief.

Gadshill   Go to, *homo* is a common name to all men: bid
the ostler bring my gelding out of the stable. Farewell,
you muddy knave.

[*Exeunt*]

Scene 2

The Highway near Gad's Hill. Enter **Prince**, **Poins** *and* **Peto**

Poins   Come, shelter, shelter! I have removed Falstaff's
horse, and he frets like a gummed velvet.

Prince   Stand close!   [*They step to one side*]

speak, rob as drink, and drink as pray. Though I tell a lie,
damn me! They pray non-stop to their saint the General
Public. Or rather, they don't pray *to* her, they prey *on* her,
'cos they take her for a ride, and flog her.

Chamberlain   What, flog the General Public? Won't she
squeal if she's whipped?

Gadshill   She will, she will. But we've got the law fixed.
We can steal in complete security, no problem. We've
got a magic formula: we walk invisible.

Chamberlain   'Strewth, your walking invisible has got more
to do with working at night than with magic!

Gadshill   Shake hands. You shall have a share of the
action. You have my word as an honest man.

Chamberlain   I'd rather you gave it me as a dishonest one.

Gadshill   Get away, we're all the same under the skin! Tell
the groom to bring my gelding out of the stable.
Farewell, bird-brain!

[*They leave*]

Scene 2

Gad's Hill: the highway. Enter **Prince, Poins** *and* **Peto**

Poins   Come on, hide! Hide! I've pinched Falstaff's horse,
and he's fretting like a man wearing a stiff collar!

Prince   Keep cover!

[*Enter* **Falstaff**]

Falstaff   Poins! Poins, and be hanged! Poins!

5 **Prince**   [*Coming forward*] Peace, ye fat-kidneyed rascal,
what a brawling dost thou keep!

Falstaff   Where's Poins, Hal?

Prince   He walked up to the top of the hill; I'll go see
him.   [*Steps aside*]

10 **Falstaff**   I am accursed to rob in that thief's company; the
rascal hath removed my horse and tied him I know not
where. If I travel but four foot by the squier further afoot,
I shall break my wind. Well, I doubt not but to die a fair
death for all this, if I scape hanging for killing that rogue.
15 I have forsworn his company hourly any time this two and
twenty years, and yet I am bewitched with the rogue's
company. If the rascal have not given me medicines to
make me love him, I'll be hanged. It could not be else, I
have drunk medicines. Poins! Hal! A plague upon you
20 both! Bardolph! Peto! I'll starve ere I'll rob a foot further – and 'twere not as good a deed as drink to turn true
man, and to leave these rogues, I am the veriest varlet that
ever chewed with a tooth: eight yards of uneven ground is
threescore and ten miles afoot with me, and the stony-hearted
25 villains know it well enough. A plague upon it
when thieves cannot be true one to another! [*They whistle*]
Whew! A plague upon you all, give me my horse, you
rogues, give me my horse and be hanged!

Prince   [*Coming forward*] Peace, ye fat guts, lie down, lay
30 thine ear close to the ground, and list if thou canst hear
the tread of travellers.

[*They conceal themselves*]

[*Enter* **Falstaff**]

Falstaff   Poins! Poins and be hanged to you! Poins!

Prince   [*showing himself*] Quiet, you fat-gutted rascal! What a row you are making!

Falstaff   Where's Poins, Hal?

Prince   He has walked to the top of the hill. I'll go and find him.

[*He leaves*]

Falstaff   It's my bad luck to be robbing in that thief's company. The rascal has taken my horse, and tied him who-knows-where. If I walk just another four feet on my two feet, I'll be knackered. If I don't get myself hanged for killing that rogue, I'll surely die a natural death. I've sworn to have done with him every hour for the last twenty-two years, but I'm bewitched by the rogue's company. I'll be hanged if the rascal hasn't drugged me to make me love him. Poins! Hal! Damn you both! Bardolph! Peto! I'll die rather than rob a foot further on. And if it wouldn't serve them right for me to turn honest, and leave the rogues, I'm the biggest idiot who ever chewed with one tooth. Eight yards of rough ground is seventy miles on foot to me, and the stony-hearted villains know it well enough. It's pretty sick when there's no honour amongst thieves. [*They whistle from a distance*] Whew! Hell and damnation! Give me my horse, you rogues, and be hanged!

Prince   [*coming from his hiding place*] Quiet, you fat guts! Lie down, put your ear close to the ground, and listen for the footsteps of travellers.

75

Falstaff   Have you any levers to lift me up again, being
   down? 'Sblood, I'll not bear my own flesh so far afoot
   again for all the coin in thy father's exchequer. What a
35   plague mean ye to colt me thus?

Prince   Thou liest, thou art not colted, thou art uncolted.

Falstaff   I prithee good Prince Hal, help me to my horse,
   good king's son.

Prince   Out, ye rogue, shall I be your ostler?

40 **Falstaff**   Hang thyself in thine own heir-apparent garters!
   If I be ta'en, I'll peach for this: and I have not ballads
   made on you all, and sung to filthy tunes, let a cup of sack
   be my poison – when a jest is so forward, and afoot too! I
   hate it.

[*Enter* **Gadshill** *and* **Bardolph**]

45 **Gadshill**   Stand!

Falstaff   So I do, against my will.

Poins   O, 'tis our setter, I know his voice.

[*Coming forward with* **Peto**]

   Bardolph, what news?

Bardolph   Case ye, case ye, on with your vizards, there's
50   money of the King's coming down the hill, 'tis going to
   the King's exchequer.

Falstaff   You lie, ye rogue, 'tis going to the King's tavern.

Gadshill   There's enough to make us all.

Falstaff   To be hanged.

55 **Prince**   Sirs, you four shall front them in the narrow lane:

Falstaff   Have you got block and tackle to lift me up again, once I'm down? God, I'll not carry my body so far afield again for all the money in your father's Exchequer. What the hell do you mean by setting me up like this?

Prince   Liar! You're not set up. You're set down!

Falstaff   Please, good Prince Hal, help me find my horse, good king's son . . .

Prince   Get away with you, you rogue! Shall I be your groom?

Falstaff   Go hang yourself in your princely Order of the Garter, since you're the heir-apparent! If I'm run in, I'll turn King's Evidence on this. May a tankard of wine be my poison if I don't have scurrilous songs made about you, and sung to filthy tunes! Just when the joke is so promising, and so far advanced, too!

[*Enter* **Gadshill** *and* **Bardolph**]

Gadshill   Stand and deliver!

Falstaff   [*rising with difficulty*] So I do, against my will.

Poins   Oh, it's our inside-man. I know his voice. [*Coming out of hiding with* **Peto**] Bardolph, what's the latest?

Bardolph   Mask yourselves, mask yourselves. On with your face-masks. There's King's money coming down the hill, going to the King's Exchequer.

Falstaff   You're lying, you rogue! It's going to the King's Tavern!

Gadshill   There's enough to make us all rich!

Falstaff   Or hanged –

Prince   Gentlemen. You four will confront them in the

Ned Poins and I will walk lower – if they scape from your
encounter, then they light on us.

Peto   How many be there of them?

Gadshill   Some eight or ten.

60 **Falstaff**   'Zounds, will they not rob us?

Prince   What, a coward, Sir John Paunch?

Falstaff   Indeed, I am not John of Gaunt, your
grandfather, but yet no coward, Hal.

Prince   Well, we leave that to the proof.

65 **Poins**   Sirrah Jack, thy horse stands behind the hedge; when
thou need'st him, there thou shalt find him. Farewell, and
stand fast.

Falstaff   Now cannot I strike him, if I should be hanged.

Prince   Ned, where are our disguises?

70 **Poins**   Here, hard by, stand close.

[*Exeunt* **Prince** *and* **Poins**]

Falstaff   Now, my masters, happy man be his dole, say
I – every man to his business.

[*Enter the* **Travellers**]

First Traveller   Come, neighbour, the boy shall lead our
horses down the hill; we'll walk afoot awhile and ease
75   our legs.

Thieves   Stand!

Second Traveller   Jesus bless us!

narrow lane. Ned Poins and I will walk on lower down. If they escape from your ambush, they'll stumble on us.

Peto   How many of them are there?

Gadshill   About eight or ten.

Falstaff   God – won't they rob us?

Prince   What – are you a coward, Sir John Paunch?

Falstaff   Indeed, I'm not exactly John of Gaunt, your grandfather, but still I'm no coward, Hal.

Prince   Well, we'll leave that to be proved.

Poins   Jack lad, your horse is standing behind the hedge. When you need him, there you'll find him. 'Bye now – and stand firm!

Falstaff   [*glad to have his horse back, and all-forgiving*] I'm hanged if I could thump him now!

Prince   [*whispering*] Ned, where are our disguises?

Poins   [*whispering back*] Here, close by. Follow me.

[**Poins** *and the* **Prince** *slip away*]

Falstaff   Now, gentlemen. 'May happiness be our lot' say I. Every man to his business!

[*The* **Travellers** *enter*]

1st Traveller   Come, neighbour. The boy can lead our horses down the hill. We'll go on foot for a while, and stretch our legs.

Thieves   Stand and deliver!

2nd Traveller   Jesus bless us!

Falstaff Strike, down with them, cut the villains' throats!
Ah, whoreson caterpillars, bacon-fed knaves, they hate us
80 youth! Down with them, fleece them!

First Traveller O, we are undone, both we and ours for
ever!

Falstaff Hang ye, gorbellied knaves, are ye undone? No,
ye fat chuffs, I would your store were here! On, bacons,
85 on! What, ye knaves! young men must live. You are
grandjurors, are ye? We'll jure ye, faith.

[*Here they rob them and bind them. Exeunt*]

[*Enter the* **Prince** *and* **Poins**, *disguised*]

Prince The thieves have bound the true men; now could
thou and I rob the thieves, and go merrily to London, it
would be argument for a week, laughter for a month, and
90 a good jest for ever.

Poins Stand close! I hear them coming.

[*They retire*]

[*Enter the* **Thieves** *again*]

Falstaff Come, my masters, let us share, and then to horse
before day. And the Prince and Poins be not two arrant
cowards there's no equity stirring; there's no more valour
95 in that Poins than in a wild duck.

[*As they are sharing the* **Prince** *and* **Poins** *set upon him*]

Falstaff Rob 'em! Down with them! Cut the villains' throats! Ah, you lousy parasites, you great lumbering nit-wits! They hate us young folk! Down with 'em! Fleece 'em!

1st Traveller [*terrified*] Oh, we are done for – both us, and ours, forever!

Falstaff Be hanged, you fat-bellied bumpkins – so you're done for, are you? No way, fat wallets! I only wish all your fortunes were here! [*Beating them*] Come on, porkers, come on! What, you no-goods! Young chaps like us must live! [*Answering their protests*] Oh, so you are Grand Jurymen, are you? [**Falstaff** *helps to rob and bind the* **Travellers**] We'll 'jure' you, indeed!

[*They all leave*]

[*The* **Prince** *and* **Poins** *re-enter in their disguises*]

Prince The thieves have bound the honest men. Now you and I could rob the thieves, and go merrily off to London. It would be talk for a week, laughter for a month, and a good joke everlastingly!

Poins Keep cover! I hear them coming!

[*They hide*]

[*The* **Thieves** *re-enter*]

Falstaff Come on, gents, let's share out, and then ride off before daybreak. If the Prince and Poins aren't two rotten cowards, there's no justice. There's no more courage in that Poins than in a wild duck!

[*As they share out the booty, the* **Prince** *and* **Poins** *set on them*]

Prince   Your money!

Poins   Villains!

[*They all run away, and* **Falstaff** *after a blow or two runs away too, leaving the booty behind them*]

Prince   Got with much ease. Now merrily to horse:
The thieves are all scattered and possessed with fear
100   So strongly that they dare not meet each other;
Each takes his fellow for an officer!
Away, good Ned – Falstaff sweats to death,
And lards the lean earth as he walks along.
Were't not for laughing I should pity him.

105 **Poins**   How the fat rogue roared!

[*Exeunt*]

Scene 3

Warkworth, Northumberland. The Castle. Enter **Hotspur** *solus, reading a letter.*

Hotspur   'But, for mine own part, my lord, I could be well
contented to be there, in respect of the love I bear your
house.' He could be contented: why is he not then? In
respect of the love he bears our house: he shows in this, he
5   loves his own barn better than he loves our house. Let me
see some more. 'The purpose you undertake is dangerous' – Why, that's certain; 'tis dangerous to take a cold, to

Prince Your money!

Poins Villains!

[*They all run away, including* **Falstaff**, *after a half-hearted exchange of sword-play*]

Prince [*looking at the purses*] Taken very easily! Now let's gallop off. The thieves are all scattered, and so frightened that they daren't re-assemble. Each one mistakes the other for a law-man. Off you go, Ned! Falstaff sweats to death, and greases the bare ground as he walks along. If it weren't for laughing, I'd be sorry for him!

Poins [*with tears of laughter in his eyes*] How the fat rogue roared!

[*They go*]

Scene 3

Warkworth Castle, Northumberland. **Hotspur** *is reading a letter*

Hotspur [*quoting*] '*As for myself, I would be very pleased to be there, out of respect for the love I bear your house*'. He would be very pleased: why isn't he then? Out of respect for the love he bears our house: this letter shows he loves his own barn better than he loves our house! [*scanning the letter again*] Let me see some more. '*What you are planning is dangerous*'. Well, that's for certain!

sleep, to drink; but I tell you, my lord fool, out of this nettle, danger, we pluck this flower, safety. 'The purpose you
10 undertake is dangerous, the friends you have named
uncertain, the time itself unsorted, and your whole plot
too light, for the counterpoise of so great an opposition.'
Say you so, say you so? I say unto you again, you are a
shallow cowardly hind, and you lie: what a lack-brain is
15 this! By the Lord, our plot is a good plot, as ever was laid,
our friends true and constant: a good plot, good friends,
and full of expectation: an excellent plot, very good friends;
what a frosty-spirited rogue is this! Why, my Lord of York
commends the plot, and the general course of the action.
20 'Zounds, and I were now by this rascal I could brain him
with his lady's fan. Is there not my father, my uncle, and
myself? Lord Edmund Mortimer, my Lord of York, and
Owen Glendower? Is there not besides the Douglas? Have
I not all their letters to meet me in arms by the ninth of
25 the next month, and are they not some of them set forward already? What a pagan rascal is this, an infidel! Ha!
You shall see now in very sincerity of fear and cold heart
will he to the King, and lay open all our proceedings! O, I
could divide myself, and go to buffets, for moving such a
30 dish of skim milk with so honourable an action! Hang
him, let him tell the King, we are prepared: I will set forward tonight.

[*Enter* **Lady Percy**]

How now, Kate? I must leave you within these two hours.

35 **Lady Percy**   O my good lord, why are you thus alone?
For what offence have I this fortnight been
A banished woman from my Harry's bed?

It's dangerous to take a cold, to sleep, to drink. But I tell you this, my Lord Fool: danger is a kind of nettle, but by grasping it firmly we ensure our safety, and turn it into a flower. '*The purpose you undertake is dangerous, the friends you have named are unreliable, the time itself is ill-chosen, and your whole plot too insubstantial to outweigh so great an opposition*'. Oh, yes? Really? I say to you again: you are a shallow, cowardly menial, and you lie! What a numbskull this one is! By the Lord Almighty, our plot is as good a plot as ever was laid. Our friends are true and constant. It's a good plot, good friends, and full of promise. An excellent plot. Very good friends. What a cold-comfort rogue this is! Why, the Archbishop of York endorses the plot, and the general plan of campaign. God! If I were now standing beside this rascal, I'd brain him with his lady-wife's fan. Is there not my father, my uncle, and myself? Lord Edmund Mortimer, my Lord of York, and Owen Glendower? Is there not Douglas in addition? Haven't I had all their letters agreeing to meet me fully mobilized by the ninth of next month, and haven't some of them set off already? What a faithless rascal this is: a real infidel! Ha! Now you'll see him going off to the King, through genuine fear and cold-heartedness, and revealing all our plans. Oh, I could split myself in two, and have one half fight the other, for putting such an honourable enterprise before such a bowl of skimmed milk as he is! Hang him! Let him tell the King! We are prepared. I'll set off tonight!

[*Enter* **Lady Percy**]

How goes it, Kate? I must leave you within a couple of hours.

Lady Percy Oh, my good lord: why are you alone like this? What have I done to deserve being a woman banished

85

Tell me, sweet lord, what is't that takes from thee
Thy stomach, pleasure, and thy golden sleep?
Why dost thou bend thine eyes upon the earth,
40   And start so often when thou sit'st alone?
Why hast thou lost the fresh blood in thy cheeks,
And given my treasures and my rights of thee
To thick-eyed musing, and curst melancholy?
In thy faint slumbers I by thee have watched,
45   And heard thee murmur tales of iron wars,
Speak terms of manage to thy bounding steed,
Cry 'Courage! To the field!' And thou hast talked
Of sallies, and retires, of trenches, tents,
Of palisadoes, frontiers, parapets,
50   Of basilisks, of cannon, culverin,
Of prisoners' ransom, and of soldiers slain,
And all the currents of a heady fight.
Thy spirit within thee hath been so at war,
And thus hath so bestirred thee in thy sleep,
55   That beads of sweat have stood upon thy brow
Like bubbles in a late-disturbed stream,
And in thy face strange motions have appeared,
Such as we see when men restrain their breath
On some great sudden hest. O, what portents are these?
60   Some heavy business hath my lord in hand,
And I must know it, else he loves me not.

Hotspur What ho!

[*Enter a* **Servant**]

                     Is Gilliams with the packet gone?

Servant He is, my lord, an hour ago.

Hotspur Hath Butler brought those horses from the
sheriff?

65 **Servant** One horse, my lord, he brought even now.

from my husband's bed? Tell me, sweet lord: what has
put you off your food, your pleasure, and your carefree
sleep? Why do you look down, and jump so often when
you're sitting alone? Why do you look so pale and
exchange my wifely comforts for ill-tempered
contemplation and peevish melancholy? I have lain
awake at your side during your light sleep, and heard you
murmuring about tough wars, – using riding-language to
your galloping horse, crying 'Courage! To the field!' And
you've talked of advances and retreats, of trenches,
tents, stakes, ramparts, defences, big guns, cannons,
field guns, of prisoners' ransoms, of soldiers killed, and
all the paraphernalia of battle. You've been so much at
war inside yourself, and it has so much disturbed you in
your sleep, that beads of sweat like bubbles in a stirred-
up stream have stood out on your forehead. And your
face-muscles have flexed, as they do when men hold
their breath on suddenly making an important decision.
What does all this mean? My Lord is involved in
something very serious: I must know what, or he doesn't
love me.

Hotspur   [*ignoring her*] Hey, there!

[*A* **Servant** *enters*]

Has Gilliams gone with the packet?

Servant   He has, my lord, an hour ago.

Hotspur   Has Butler brought those horses from the sheriff?

Servant   He brought one just now, my lord.

Hotspur   What horse? A roan, a crop-ear is it not?

Servant   It is, my lord.

Hotspur   That roan shall be my throne.
　　Well, I will back him straight: O Esperance!
　　Bid Butler lead him forth into the park.

> [*Exit* **Servant**]

70 **Lady Percy**   But hear you, my lord.

Hotspur   What say'st thou, my lady?

Lady Percy   What is it carries you away?

Hotspur   Why, my horse, my love, my horse.

Lady Percy   Out, you mad-headed ape!
75 　　A weasel hath not such a deal of spleen
　　As you are tossed with. In faith,
　　I'll know your business, Harry, that I will;
　　I fear my brother Mortimer doth stir
　　About his title, and hath sent for you
80 　　To line his enterprise. But if you go –

Hotspur   So far afoot I shall be weary, love.

Lady Percy   Come, come, you paraquito, answer me
　　Directly unto this question that I ask;
　　In faith, I'll break thy little finger, Harry,
85 　　And if thou wilt not tell me all things true.

Hotspur   Away,
　　Away, you trifler! Love! I love thee not,
　　I care not for thee, Kate; this is no world
　　To play with mammets, and to tilt with lips;
90 　　We must have bloody noses, and cracked crowns,
　　And pass them current too. God's me! my horse!
　　What say'st thou, Kate? What wouldst thou have with me?

Hotspur   Which horse? A roan? The crop-eared one?

Servant   It is, my lord.

Hotspur   That roan will be my throne. Well, I'll mount him right away. 'Hope be my comfort'! Tell Butler to lead him out into the grounds.

[*The* **Servant** *goes*]

Lady Percy   But listen to me, my lord!

Hotspur   [*turning to her at last*] What's that you say dear?

Lady Percy   What is it that's carrying you away?

Hotspur   Why, my horse, my love, my horse!

Lady Percy   Get away, you mad-headed ape! A weasel is better tempered than you are! Now then: I'll know your business, Harry, that I will! I fear my brother, Mortimer, is making a bid for the succession, and has sent for you to add strength to his venture. But if you go –

Hotspur   [*finishing her sentence for her, mischievously*] – So far on foot, I'll be weary, love.

Lady Percy   Come on, you parrot! Give me a direct answer to my question! Indeed, I'll break your little finger if you don't tell me the whole truth. [*She tries to seize his hand*]

Hotspur   [*pushing her off, amused*] Off – get off, you pest! Love? I don't love you! I have no fondness for you, Kate. This isn't a world for playing with dolls, and jousting with lips. It's bloody noses for us, and fractured crowns. They must be our currency. God bless me, where's my horse? [*Deliberately awkward*] What was it you said Kate? What did you want?

Lady Percy Do you not love me? Do you not indeed?
Well, do not then, for since you love me not
95 I will not love myself. Do you not love me?
Nay, tell me if you speak in jest or no.

Hotspur Come, wilt thou see me ride?
And when I am a-horseback I will swear
I love thee infinitely. But hark you, Kate,
100 I must not have you henceforth question me
Whither I go, nor reason whereabout:
Whither I must, I must; and, to conclude,
This evening must I leave you, gentle Kate.
I know you wise, but yet no farther wise
105 Than Harry Percy's wife; constant you are,
But yet a woman; and for secrecy
No lady closer, for I well believe
Thou wilt not utter what thou dost not know;
And so far will I trust thee, gentle Kate.

110 **Lady Percy** How? so far?

Hotspur Not an inch further. But hark you, Kate,
Whither I go, thither shall you go too:
Today will I set forth, tomorrow you.
Will this content you, Kate?

Lady Percy   It must, of force.

[Exeunt]

Lady Percy   [*peeved*] Don't you love me? Don't you really? Well then, don't! Since you don't love me, I won't love myself. [*Worried*] Don't you love me? Please, tell me if you're joking or not . . .

Hotspur   Come on, will you see me off? When I'm on horseback, I'll swear I love you infinitely. But listen, Kate: I can't have you questioning me in future where I go, or guessing why. Where I have to go, I have to go. So to sum up, I must leave you this evening, gentle Kate. I know you are very sensible; but only as sensible as Harry Percy's *wife*. You are loyal, but nonetheless a woman. As for secrecy, there's no woman more tight-lipped: you can't tell what you don't know. And that's how far I'll trust you, gentle Kate.

Lady Percy   Really? [*sarcastically*] So far?

Hotspur   Not an inch further. But listen, Kate. Where I go, there you shall go too. I'll set off today, you can depart tomorrow. Will that satisfy you, Kate?

Lady Percy   It must, of necessity . . .

[*They leave together*]

Scene 4

Eastcheap. The Boar's Head Tavern. Enter **Prince** *and* **Poins.**

Prince   Ned, prithee come out of that fat room, and lend
me thy hand to laugh a little.

Poins   Where hast been, Hal?

5 **Prince**   With three or four loggerheads, amongst three or
fourscore hogsheads. I have sounded the very basestring of
humility. Sirrah, I am sworn brother to a leash of drawers,
and can call them all by their christen names, as Tom,
Dick and Francis. They take it already upon their
salvation, that though I be but Prince of Wales, yet I am
10 the king of courtesy, and tell me flatly I am no proud
Jack like Falstaff, but a Corinthian, a lad of mettle, a good
boy (by the Lord, so they call me!), and when I am King
of England I shall command all the good lads in Eastcheap. They call drinking deep dyeing scarlet, and when
15 you breathe in your watering they cry 'Hem!' and bid you
'Play it off'. To conclude, I am so good a proficient in
one quarter of an hour that I can drink with any tinker in
his own language during my life. I tell thee, Ned, thou
hast lost much honour that thou wert not with me in this
20 action; but, sweet Ned – to sweeten which name of Ned I
give thee this pennyworth of sugar, clapped even now into
my hand by an underskinker, one that never spake other
English in his life than 'Eight shillings and sixpence', and
'You are welcome', with this shrill addition, 'Anon, anon,
25 sir! Score a pint of bastard in the Half-moon', or so. But
Ned, to drive away the time till Falstaff come:- I prithee do
thou stand in some by-room, while I question my puny
drawer to what end he gave me the sugar, and do thou
never leave calling 'Francis!', that his tale to me may be

Scene 4

The Boar's Head Tavern at Eastcheap. Enter the **Prince** *and*
Poins

Prince   Ned, come out of that stuffy room, and lend me a
hand to laugh a bit!

Poins   Where've you been, Hal?

Prince   With three or four clots amongst sixty to eighty
sots! I've struck rock bottom. D'you know, I'm blood
brother of three barmen, and can call them all by their
Christian names – Tom, Dick and Francis. They're
'blessed if I'm not the king of politeness' – in spite of
being only the Prince of Wales; and they tell me straight
I'm not a stuck up fellow like Falstaff, but 'a gay dog',
'one of the lads', 'a good boy'. Dear God! That's what
they call me! When I'm King of England, I'll have the
backing of all the good lads of Eastcheap. They call
quaffing ale 'reddening one's face', and when you pause
for a breath in the middle of a drink, they cry 'Cough it
up!' and tell you to 'Get it down!'. To cut a long story
short, I've become so skilled in a quarter of an hour that I
can drink now with any tinker as an equal for the rest of
my life. Honestly, Ned, you've lost a lot of credit for
missing this appointment. But however, sweet Ned . . .
to sweeten that name of Ned, I give you this penn'orth of
sugar, slapped into my hand by a pot-boy, who never
spoke more English in his life than 'Forty-five pence!' and
'You're very welcome!' – with the high-pitched addition
of 'Coming, coming sir! Put a pint of wine on the slate in
the Half-moon Room' and so on. But Ned . . . to pass the
time till Falstaff comes, do me a favour and stand in
some side-room, while I question this inexperienced pot-
boy as to why he gave me the sugar. Don't stop calling

30   nothing but 'Anon'. Step aside, and I'll show thee a
      precedent.

                                                    [**Poins** *retires*]

    Poins   [*Within*] Francis!

    Prince   Thou art perfect.

    Poins   [*Within*] Francis!

      [*Enter* **Francis**, *a Drawer*]

35 **Francis**   Anon, anon, sir. Look down into the Pomgarnet,
      Ralph.

    Prince   Come hither, Francis.

    Francis   My lord?

    Prince   How long hast thou to serve, Francis?

40 **Francis**   Forsooth, five years, and as much as to –

    Poins   [*Within*] Francis!

    Francis   Anon, anon, sir.

    Prince   Five year! By'r lady, a long lease for the clinking of
      pewter; but Francis, darest thou be so valiant as to play the
45   coward with thy indenture, and show it a fair pair of
      heels, and run from it?

    Francis   O Lord, sir, I'll be sworn upon all the books in
      England, I could find in my heart –

    Poins   [*Within*] Francis!

50 **Francis**   Anon, sir.

    Prince   How old art thou, Francis?

out 'Francis!' so that all he'll say is 'Coming!' Step to one side, and I'll give you an example.

[**Poins** *moves to the next room*]

Poins   [*from the room*] Francis!

Prince   Just right!

Poins   Francis!

[*Enter* **Francis***, a pot-boy*]

Francis   Coming, sir! Coming! [*To a fellow-waiter*] Just check the Pomegranate Room, Ralph.

Prince   Come here, Francis!

Francis   My lord?

Prince   How many more years of your apprenticeship have you to serve, Francis?

Francis   Actually, five years, and as much as to –

Poins   Francis!

Francis   [*over his shoulder*] Coming! Coming sir!

Prince   Five years! My word, a long stretch for the clinking of tankards. But Francis, have you got the courage to treat your apprenticeship cowardly, and show it a clean pair of heels by running away from it?

Francis   Oh lord, sir! I'd swear on all the bibles in England that I could find it in my heart –

Poins   [*loudly*] Francis!

Francis   Coming, sir!

Prince   How old are you, Francis?

Francis   Let me see, about Michaelmas next I shall be –

Poins   [*Within*] Francis!

Francis   Anon, sir. Pray stay a little, my lord.

55 **Prince**   Nay but hark you, Francis, for the sugar thou
gavest me, 'twas a pennyworth, was't not?

Francis   O Lord, I would it had been two!

Prince   I will give thee for it a thousand pound – ask me
when thou wilt, and thou shalt have it.

60 **Poins**   [*Within*] Francis!

Francis   Anon, anon.

Prince   Anon, Francis? No, Francis, but tomorrow, Francis;
or, Francis, a-Thursday; or indeed, Francis, when thou
wilt. But Francis!

65 **Francis**   My lord?

Prince   Wilt thou rob this leathern-jerkin, crystal-button,
not-pated, agate-ring, puke-stocking, caddis-garter,
smooth-tongue Spanish pouch?

Francis   O Lord, sir, who do you mean?

70 **Prince**   Why then your brown bastard is your only drink:
for look you, Francis, your white canvas doublet will
sully. In Barbary, sir, it cannot come to so much.

Francis   What, sir?

Francis   [*looking apprehensively at the door, but answering the* **Prince** *courteously*] Let me see, about the end of next September I'll be . . .

Poins   [*getting louder and angrier*] Francis!

Francis   Coming, sir! Could you wait a moment, my lord?

Prince   No, but listen, Francis. About that sugar you gave me. It was a pennyworth, wasn't it?

Francis   [*distressed, not being able to get away*] Oh lord! Two for all it matters!

Prince   I'll give you a thousand pounds for it. Ask me whenever you want. You can have it.

Poins   [*exploding*] Francis!

Francis   [*agitated even more*] Coming, coming soon!

Prince   [*talking very rapidly, to the confusion of poor* **Francis**] Soon, Francis? No, Francis. Maybe tomorrow, Francis. Or Francis – on Thursday; or indeed Francis, whenever you want. But Francis –

Francis   [*trembling now*] My lord?

Prince   [*referring to the* **Innkeeper**] Would you rob this leather-jacketed, pearl-buttoned, short-haired, agate-ringed, wool-stockinged, worsted-gartered, smooth-tongued, leather-pursed –

Francis   [*totally bewildered and terrified*] Oh lord, Sir, what do you mean?

Prince   [*relentlessly confusing*] Well, then, serving brown ale's your only hope, 'cos think, Francis – your white canvas coat will soon get dirty. Barbary sugar, sir, couldn't cost so much!

Francis   What, sir?

97

Poins   [*Within*] Francis!

75 **Prince**   Away, you rogue, dost thou not hear them call?

[*Here they both call him; the Drawer stands amazed, not knowing which way to go*]

[*Enter* **Vintner**]

Vintner   What, stand'st thou still and hear'st such a calling? Look to the guests within. [*Exit* **Francis**] My lord, old Sir John with half-a-dozen more are at the door. Shall I let them in?

80 **Prince**   Let them alone awhile, and then open the door.

[*Exit* **Vintner**]

Poins!

[*Re-enter* **Poins**]

Poins   Anon, anon, sir.

Prince   Sirrah, Falstaff and the rest of the thieves are at the door. Shall we be merry?

85 **Poins**   As merry as crickets, my lad; but hark ye, what cunning match have you made with this jest of the drawer: come, what's the issue?

Prince   I am now of all humours that have showed themselves humours since the old days of goodman Adam
90   to the pupil age of this present twelve o'clock at midnight.

[*Re-enter* **Francis**]

What's o'clock, Francis?

Poins   [*loudly*] Francis!

Prince   Get away with you! Don't you hear them calling you?

[*At this point, both* **Poins** *and the* **Prince** *call* **Francis**, *and he stands quivering between them like an ass between two bales of hay, not knowing which way to turn*]

[*Enter the* **Innkeeper**]

Innkeeper   What are you standing there for, when you're being called? Attend to the guests in the rooms! [*Exit* **Francis**, *blubbering*] My lord, old Sir John and half-a-dozen others are at the door. Shall I let them in?

Prince   Keep them waiting a bit, then open up. Poins!

[*The* **Innkeeper** *leaves*]

[**Poins** *enters*]

Poins   Coming! Coming, sir!

Prince   Falstaff and the rest of the thieves are at the door. Shall we have some fun?

Poins   We'll be as merry as crickets, lad! But listen, what's the point of all this larking with the pot-boy? What's the game?

Prince   There's no form of amusement ever invented, from the dawn of creation till this very day, that I'm not ready for now!

[*Enter* **Francis**. *The* **Prince** *winks at* **Poins**]

What's the time, Francis?

Francis   Anon, anon, sir.

[*Exit*]

Prince   That ever this fellow should have fewer words than
a parrot, and yet the son of a woman! His industry is
95   up-stairs and down-stairs, his eloquence the parcel of a
reckoning. I am not yet of Percy's mind, the Hotspur of
the north, he that kills me some six or seven dozen of
Scots at a breakfast, washes his hands, and says to his
wife, 'Fie upon this quiet life, I want work'. 'O my sweet
100   Harry', says she, 'how many hast thou killed today?' 'Give
my roan horse a drench', says he, and answers, 'Some
fourteen', an hour after; 'a trifle, a trifle'. I prithee call in
Falstaff; I'll play Percy, and that damned brawn shall play
Dame Mortimer, his wife. Rivo! says the drunkard: call in
105   Ribs, call in Tallow.

[*Enter* **Falstaff**, **Gadshill**, **Bardolph**, *and* **Peto**; *followed
by* **Francis**, *with wine*]

Poins   Welcome, Jack, where hast thou been?

Falstaff   A plague of all cowards, I say, and a vengeance
too, marry and amen! Give me a cup of sack, boy. Ere I
lead this life long, I'll sew netherstocks, and mend them
110   and foot them too. A plague of all cowards! Give me a cup
of sack, rogue; is there no virtue extant?

[*He drinketh*]

Prince   Didst thou never see Titan kiss a dish of butter
(pitiful-hearted Titan!), that melted at the sweet tale of the
sun's? If thou didst, then behold that compound.

Francis   [*still flustered*] Coming! Coming sir! [*He rushes off*]

Prince   How can he be the son of a woman and yet know fewer words than a parrot? His life is all upstairs, downstairs; his speech nothing but adding up bills. [*He yawns*] I'm not like that Percy fellow – the Hotspur of the North – the one that kills six or seven dozen Scots before breakfast, washes his hands, then says to his wife 'To hell with this quiet life! I want some real fighting!' 'Oh my darling Harry', she says, 'how many have you killed today?' 'Give my roan horse a drink!' he says, and replies 'About fourteen'; and then, an hour later 'a mere nothing, a mere nothing'. Call in Falstaff. I'll play the part of Percy, and that damned fat boar can play Dame Mortimer, his wife. 'Drink deep!' says the drunkard. Call in Meat! Call in Fat!

[**Poins** *opens the door and admits* **Falstaff, Gadshill, Bardolph** *and* **Peto**, *followed by* **Francis** *carrying a tray of wine*]

Poins   Welcome Jack. [*All innocence*] Where have you been?

Falstaff   May the plague take all cowards, that's what I say! And a vengeance, too! Amen to that! [*To* **Francis**] Give me a tankard of wine, boy. Rather than live this kind of life any longer, I'll knit stockings, and mend them, and re-foot them too. A plague on all cowards! [*Beckoning to* **Francis** *again*] Give me a tankard of wine, rogue! Is there no honesty any more? [*He drinks deeply, not pausing for breath*]

Prince   [*commenting wittily on* **Falstaff's** *face as he drinks*] Did you ever see anything more like the sun melting a dish of butter?

115 **Falstaff** You rogue, here's lime in this sack too: there is
nothing but roguery to be found in villainous man, yet a
coward is worse than a cup of sack with lime in it. A villainous coward! Go thy ways, old Jack, die when thou wilt;
if manhood, good manhood, be not forgot upon the face of

120 the earth, then am I a shotten herring: there lives not three
good men unhanged in England, and one of them is fat,
and grows old, God help the while! A bad world, I say. I
would I were a weaver; I could sing psalms, or anything. A
plague of all cowards, I say still!

125 **Prince** How now, wool-sack, what mutter you?

Falstaff A king's son! If I do not beat thee out of thy
kingdom with a dagger of lath, and drive all thy subjects
afore thee like a flock of wild geese, I'll never wear hair on
my face more. You, Prince of Wales!

130 **Prince** Why, you whoreson round man, what's the matter?

Falstaff Are not you a coward? Answer me to that – and
Poins there?

Poins 'Zounds, ye fat paunch, and ye call me coward by
the Lord I'll stab thee.

135 **Falstaff** I call thee coward? I'll see thee damned ere I call
thee coward, but I would give a thousand pound I could
run as fast as thou canst. You are straight enough in the
shoulders, you care not who sees your back: call you that
backing of your friends? A plague upon such backing, give

140 me them that will face me! Give me a cup of sack: I am a
rogue if I drunk today.

Falstaff [*lowering the tankard as he empties it, and wiping his mouth. He addresses* **Francis**] You rogue! This wine has been treated! Men are nothing but out-and-out rogues! But a coward is worse than doctored wine! A villainous coward! Off you go, old Jack; die when you're ready. If manliness, decent manliness, hasn't disappeared from this world, then I'm a tiddler! There are only three good men left in England unhanged, and one of them is fat, and grows old, God help us! It's a bad world, I say! I wish I were one of those bible-punching weavers, then I could sing some psalms, or something. A plague on all cowards, I still say!

Prince What's that, stuffed-sack? What are you muttering?

Falstaff And you a King's son! If I don't beat you out of your kingdom with a clown's wooden sword, and drive all your subjects in front of you like a flock of wild geese, I'll never grow another beard. [*Scornfully*] You, Prince of Wales!

Prince Why, you fat old reprobate, what's the matter?

Falstaff Aren't you a coward? Answer me that? And Poins there, too?

Poins Watch it, you fat guts! If you call me a coward, by God I'll stab you!

Falstaff I call you a coward? I'll see you damned before I'd call you a coward! But I'd give a thousand pounds to be able to run as fast as you can. You've got a fair pair of shoulders: you don't mind who sees your back. Do you call that 'backing up your friends'? To hell with such backing; give me the man who'll face me! Give me a tankard of wine. I'm damned if I've had a drink all day.

Prince   O villain! Thy lips are scarce wiped since thou
drunk'st last.

Falstaff   All is one for that. [*He drinketh*] A plague of all
145   cowards, still say I.

Prince   What's the matter?

Falstaff   What's the matter? There be four of us here have
ta'en a thousand pound this day morning.

Prince   Where is it, Jack, where is it?

150 **Falstaff**   Where is it? Taken from us it is: a hundred upon
poor four of us.

Prince   What, a hundred, man?

Falstaff   I am a rogue if I were not at half-sword with a
dozen of them two hours together. I have scaped by mira-
155   cle. I am eight times thrust through the doublet, four
through the hose, my buckler cut through and through,
my sword hacked like a handsaw – *ecce signum*! I never
dealt better since I was a man: all would not do. A plague
of all cowards! Let them speak – if they speak more or less
160   than truth, they are villains, and the sons of darkness.

Prince   Speak, sirs, how was it?

Gadshill   We four set upon some dozen –

Falstaff   Sixteen at least, my lord.

Gadshill   And bound them.

165 **Peto**   No, no, they were not bound.

Falstaff   You rogue, they were bound, every man of them,
or I am a Jew else: an Ebrew Jew.

Prince   Villain! You've scarcely wiped your lips since you last drank!

Falstaff   Be that as it may! [*He drinks deeply again*] A plague on all cowards, I still say!

Prince   What's the matter?

Falstaff   What's the matter? Four of us here took a thousand pounds this morning.

Prince   Where is it, Jack? Where is it?

Falstaff   Where is it? Taken from us, it was. A hundred ambushed poor four of us.

Prince   What, a hundred, man?

Falstaff   Call me a rogue if I wasn't in hand-to-hand fighting with a dozen of them for fully two hours. I've escaped by a miracle. I've been stabbed through the jacket eight times, and through my breeches four times; my shield has been cut through and through; and the edge of my sword looks like a hacksaw. Here's the proof! [*He produces a tattered-looking short sword*] I've never fought better in my life. Normal wasn't good enough. A plague on all cowards! Let them say their say [*pointing to his thieving companions*]: if they speak anything more or less than the truth, they are villains, and damned.

Prince   [*turning to them*] Speak, gentlemen. How was it?

Gadshill   We four set upon some dozen –

Falstaff   Sixteen at least, my lord –

Gadshill   And bound them.

Peto   No, no – they weren't bound . . .

Falstaff   You rogue, they were bound, every man of them, or else I'm a no-good Jew – a Hebrew Jew!

Gadshill   As we were sharing, some six or seven fresh men
set upon us –

170 **Falstaff**   And unbound the rest, and then come in the
other.

Prince   What, fought you with them all?

Falstaff   All? I know not what you call all, but if I fought
not with fifty of them I am a bunch of radish: if there were
175   not two or three and fifty upon poor old Jack, then am I
no two-legged creature.

Prince   Pray God you have not murdered some of them.

Falstaff   Nay, that's past praying for, I have peppered two
of them. Two I am sure I have paid, two rogues in buck-
180   ram suits. I tell thee what, Hal, if I tell thee a lie, spit in
my face, call me horse. Thou knowest my old ward – here
I lay, and thus I bore my point. Four rogues in buckram
let drive at me –

Prince   What, four? Thou saidst but two even now.

185 **Falstaff**   Four, Hal, I told thee four.

Poins   Ay, ay, he said four.

Falstaff   These four came all afront, and mainly thrust at
me; I made me no more ado, but took all their seven points
in my target, thus!

190 **Prince**   Seven? Why, there were but four even now.

Falstaff   In buckram?

Poins   Ay, four, in buckram suits.

Falstaff   Seven, by these hilts, or I am a villain else.

Gadshill   As we were sharing out, some six or seven fresh men jumped on us –

Falstaff   – And unbound the first lot, who joined with the others –

Prince   What, did you fight with them all?

Falstaff   All? I don't know what you call 'all', but if I didn't fight with fifty of them, then I'm a bunch of radish. If there weren't fifty-two or fifty-three on poor old Jack, then I'm no two-legged creature.

Prince   I hope to God you haven't murdered any of them?

Falstaff   Nay, you're too late. I've riddled two of them. I'm sure I've put paid to two. I tell you what, Hal, if I'm lying, spit on my face and call me horse! You know my old defensive style. [*He demonstrates by gesturing in the air*]: here's how I took my guard, and this way I pointed my sword. Four rogues dressed in buckram suits came at me –

Prince   What, four? You said only two just now.

Falstaff   Four, Hal. I told you four.

Poins   Yes, yes, he said four.

Falstaff   These four came abreast, and they thrust at me with might and main. I did no more than simply take their seven sword-tips on my shield, like this . . . [*He demonstrates with a forward jab*]

Prince   Seven? Why, there were only four just now.

Falstaff   In buckram?

Poins   Yes – four in buckram suits.

Falstaff   Seven, I swear by this hilt [*slapping his sword*], or else I'm a villain.

107

Prince   Prithee let him alone, we shall have more anon.

195 **Falstaff**   Dost thou hear me, Hal?

Prince   Ay, and mark thee too, Jack.

Falstaff   Do so, for it is worth the listening to. These nine in buckram that I told thee of –

Prince   So, two more already.

200 **Falstaff**   Their points being broken –

Poins   Down fell their hose.

Falstaff   Began to give me ground; but I followed me close, came in, foot and hand, and, with a thought, seven of the eleven I paid.

205 **Prince**   O monstrous! Eleven buckram men grown out of two!

Falstaff   But as the devil would have it, three misbegotten knaves in Kendal green came at my back and let drive at me, for it was so dark, Hal, that thou couldst not see thy
210   hand.

Prince   These lies are like their father that begets them, gross as a mountain, open, palpable. Why, thou clay-brained guts, thou knotty-patted fool, thou whoreson obscene greasy tallow-catch, –

215 **Falstaff**   What, art thou mad? art thou mad? Is not the truth the truth?

Prince   Why, how couldst thou know these men in Kendal green when it was so dark thou couldst not see thy hand?

Prince   [*aside to* **Poins**] Do let him go on; we'll have more soon!

Falstaff   Are you listening, Hal?

Prince   Yes, and taking careful note, too, Jack . . .

Falstaff   Do so, because it's worth listening to. [*Resuming*] These nine in buckram that I told you about –

Prince   Oh, two more already!

Falstaff   – Their points having snapped –

Poins   [*flicking his own 'points', or braces*] Down fell their breeches!

Falstaff   [*ignoring him and carrying on*] – they began to fall back. But I followed through closely. Then I attacked; foot forward, hand outstretched [*he shows the action dramatically*], and quick as a flash, I'd done for seven of the eleven.

Prince   Oh, how monstrous! Eleven buckram men have now grown out of two!

Falstaff   But, trust the devil, three misbegotten knaves dressed in Kendal green came behind me and let drive. D'you know, it was so dark, Hal, that you couldn't see your hand.

Prince   These lies are like their begetter, huge as a mountain, openly obvious, and plain to see. Why, you clay-brained guts, you block-headed fool, you lousy, obscene, greasy lump of candle-fat –

Falstaff   What, are you mad? Are you mad? Is not the truth, the truth?

Prince   Why – how could you recognize these men in Kendal green when it was so dark you couldn't see your

109

Come, tell us your reason. What sayest thou to this?

220 **Poins**   Come, your reason, Jack, your reason.

Falstaff   What, upon compulsion? 'Zounds, and I were at
the strappado, or all the racks in the world, I would not
tell you on compulsion. Give you a reason on compulsion?
If reasons were as plentiful as blackberries, I would give
225   no man a reason upon compulsion, I.

Prince   I'll be no longer guilty of this sin. This sanguine
coward, this bed-presser, this horse-back-breaker, this
huge hill of flesh –

Falstaff   'Sblood, you starveling, you eel-skin, you dried
230   neat's-tongue, you bull's-pizzle, you stock-fish – O for
breath to utter what is like thee! – you tailor's yard, you
sheath, you bow-case, you vile standing tuck!

Prince   Well, breathe awhile, and then to it again, and
when thou hast tired thyself in base comparisons hear me
235   speak but this.

Poins   Mark, Jack.

Prince   We two saw you four set on four, and bound them
and were master of their wealth – mark now how a plain
tale shall put you down. Then did we two set on you four,
240   and, with a word, out-faced you from your prize, and
have it, yea, and can show it you here in the house: and
Falstaff, you carried your guts away as nimbly, with as
quick dexterity, and roared for mercy, and still run and
roared, as ever I heard bull-calf. What a slave art thou to

hand? Come on, give us your explanation! What do you
say to that?

Poins   Come on, your explanation, Jack, your explanation!

Falstaff   What? Under compulsion? God, if I were
undergoing cruel torture, or on all the racks of the world,
I wouldn't tell you under compulsion! Give an explanation
under compulsion? If explanations were as plentiful as
blackberries, I wouldn't give a man an explanation under
compulsion! Not me!

Prince   I mustn't sin any longer. This red-faced coward,
this bed-flattener, this breaker of horses' backs, this
huge hill of flesh –

Falstaff   [*abusing the* **Prince's** *lankiness*] God – you
skeleton, you skin-of-an-eel, you dried ox's tongue, you
bull's prick, you dried cod – oh, for the breath to utter
what you are like! – you tailor's yard, you sheath, you
bowcase, you vile upstanding rapier! [*He runs out of
puff*]

Prince   Well, take a few breaths and start again. And when
you've exhausted yourself with odious comparisons,
listen to me say merely this –

Poins   Listen, Jack!

Prince   We two [*meaning himself and* **Poins**] saw you four
[*meaning* **Falstaff** *and his companions*] set upon four
[*meaning the rich travellers*], and bind them, to seize their
wealth. Notice now how a simple story will scotch
you! Then we two set on you four and, in short, we
separated you from your booty, and we still have it: yes,
and can show it to you here in this house. And, Falstaff,
you conveyed your guts away as nimbly, and with as
sure-footed dexterity, as any bull-calf that I ever heard:
roaring for mercy, and running and roaring. What a

111

245   hack thy sword as thou hast done, and then say it was in fight! What trick, what device, what starting-hole canst thou now find out, to hide thee from this open and apparent shame?

  Poins   Come, let's hear, Jack, what trick hast thou now?

250 **Falstaff**   By the Lord, I knew ye as well as he that made ye. Why, hear you, my masters, was it for me to kill the heir–apparent? Should I turn upon the true prince? Why, thou knowest I am as valiant as Hercules: but beware instinct: the lion will not touch the true prince.
255   Instinct is a great matter. I was now a coward on instinct. I shall think the better of myself, and thee, during my life – I for a valiant lion, and thou for a true prince. But by the Lord, lads, I am glad you have the money. Hostess, clap to the doors! Watch tonight, pray tomorrow! – Gallants, lads, boys, hearts of gold, all the titles of good
260   fellowship come to you! What, shall we be merry, shall we have a play extempore?

  Prince   Content, and the argument shall be thy running away.

  Falstaff   Ah, no more of that, Hal, and thou lovest me.

  [*Enter* **Hostess**]

  Hostess   O Jesu, my lord the Prince!

265 **Prince**   How now, my lady the hostess, what say'st thou to me?

  Hostess   Marry, my lord, there is a nobleman of the court at door would speak with you: he says he comes from your father.

270 **Prince**   Give him as much as will make him a royal man, and send him back again to my mother.

wretch you are to hack your sword as you have done, and then to say it happened in a fight! What trick, what strategy, what bolt-hole can you now find to cover up this open and obvious disgrace?

Poins   Come on, let's hear it, Jack! What trick have you got now?

Falstaff   [*after the slightest of pauses*] By heavens, I knew you as well as your fathers! Now listen, sirs: was it up to me to kill the heir apparent? Should I attack the true prince? Why, you know I'm as brave as Hercules, but beware of Instinct. A lion will not attack a true prince. Instinct is very powerful. I was then a coward by Instinct. I'll think the better of myself, and you, for the rest of my life: myself, as a valiant lion; you, the true prince. But by heavens, lads, I'm glad you've got the money! Hostess, lock the doors. Make merry tonight and pray tomorrow. Sports! Lads! Boyos! Hearts of gold! May all the names given to good fellowship be yours! What, shall we have fun? Shall we have an impromptu play?

Prince   Right! And the plot shall be – your running away!

Falstaff   Ah – enough of that, Hal, for pity's sake!

[*Enter* **Hostess**]

Hostess   Oh Jesus! My lord Prince, sir –

Prince   Well now, my lady hostess, what have you to say?

Hostess   Indeed, my lord, there's a nobleman from the court at the door who wants to speak to you. He says he comes from your father.

Prince   Upgrade him to royal status and send him back to my mother!

Falstaff What manner of man is he?

Hostess An old man.

275 **Falstaff** What doth gravity out of his bed at midnight?
Shall I give him his answer?

Prince Prithee do, Jack.

Falstaff Faith, and I'll send him packing.

[*Exit*]

Prince Now, sirs: by'r lady, you fought fair, so did you,
280   Peto, so did you, Bardolph; you are lions too, you ran
away upon instinct, you will not touch the true prince, no,
fie!

Bardolph Faith, I ran when I saw others run.

Prince Faith, tell me now in earnest, how came Falstaff's
285   sword so hacked?

Peto Why, he hacked it with his dagger, and said he would
swear truth out of England but he would make you
believe it was done in fight, and persuaded us to do the
like.

290 **Bardolph** Yea, and to tickle our noses with spear-grass, to
make them bleed, and then to beslubber our garments
with it, and swear it was the blood of true men. I did that
I did not this seven year before, I blushed to hear his
monstrous devices.

295 **Prince** O villain, thou stolest a cup of sack eighteen years
ago, and wert taken with the manner, and ever since thou
hast blushed extempore. Thou hadst fire and sword on thy
side, and yet thou ran'st away – what instinct hadst thou
for it?

300 **Bardolph** My lord, do you see these meteors? Do you
behold these exhalations?

114

Falstaff   What kind of man is he?

Hostess   An old man.

Falstaff   Why is Respectability not in bed at this time of night? Shall I answer him?

Prince   Please do, Jack.

Falstaff   'Strewth – I'll send him packing! [*He leaves*]

Prince   Now, gentlemen: by all that's holy, you fought fair. You did, Peto, and so did you, Bardolph. You are lions, too – you ran away upon Instinct. You wouldn't touch the true prince, oh no!

Bardolph   'Strewth, I ran when I saw the others run.

Prince   [*mocking*] 'Strewth, tell me the honest truth now – how did Falstaff's sword come to be so hacked?

Peto   Why, he hacked it with his dagger, and said he would swear blind it was done in fighting, and make you believe it. He persuaded us to do to the same.

Bardolph   Yes, and to tickle our noses with couch-grass to make them bleed, and then smear our garments with it, and swear it was the blood of valiant men. I did what I haven't done these seven years: I blushed when I heard his shameful schemes.

Prince   [*pointing to* **Bardolph's** *fiery features*] Villain! You stole a tankard of wine eighteen years ago, and you were caught 'red-faced'. Ever since, you've blushed naturally. You had this fire – and your sword – on your side, and yet you ran away. What was the instinct behind that?

Bardolph   [*pointing to his boils and pimples*] My lord, do you see these meteors? Do you behold these shooting stars?

Prince   I do.

Bardolph   What think you they portend?

Prince   Hot livers, and cold purses.

305 **Bardolph**   Choler, my lord, if rightly taken.

Prince   No, if rightly taken, halter.

[*Enter* **Falstaff**]

Here comes lean Jack, here comes bare-bone. How now,
my sweet creature of bombast, how long is't ago, Jack,
since thou sawest thine own knee?

310 **Falstaff**   My own knee? When I was about thy years, Hal,
I was not an eagle's talon in the waist, I could have crept
into any alderman's thumb-ring: a plague of sighing and
grief, it blows a man up like a bladder. There's villainous
news abroad: here was Sir John Bracy from your father;
315 you must to the court in the morning. That same mad
fellow of the north, Percy, and he of Wales that gave
Amamon the bastinado, and made Lucifer cuckold, and
swore the devil his true liegeman upon the cross of a
Welsh hook – what a plague call you him?

320 **Poins**   O, Glendower.

Falstaff   Owen, Owen, the same; and his son-in-law
Mortimer, and old Northumberland, and that sprightly
Scot of Scots, Douglas, that runs a-horseback up a hill
perpendicular –

325 **Prince**   He that rides at high speed, and with his pistol kills
a sparrow flying.

Falstaff   You have hit it.

116

Prince   I do.

Bardolph   What do you think they signify?

Prince   Ruined livers and empty pockets.

Bardolph   Choler, my lord: aggressiveness, if taken rightly.

Prince   No! if taken rightly – a collar from the hangman!

[*Enter* **Falstaff**]

Here comes skinny Jack, here comes spare-ribs! Well
now, my dear bag of wind; how long ago is it, Jack,
since you saw your own knee?

Falstaff   My own knee? When I was about your age, Hal, I
wasn't any more than an eagle's claw round the waist. I
could have slipped through an alderman's signet ring. To
hell with sighing and grief; it blows a man up like a
balloon! There's very bad news going round. That was
Sir John Bracy, from your father. You must go to Court
tomorrow morning. The mad fellow from the North –
Harry Percy – and that Welshman who claims he
thrashed the devil, gave Lucifer his horns, and got him to
swear allegiance using a Welsh bill-hook for a cross –
what the plague's his name? –

Poins   Oh . . . Glendower?

Falstaff   Owen, Owen – that's the one. And his son-in-law
Mortimer, and old Northumberland, and that sprightly
super-Scot, Douglas, who can ride up perpendicular hills
on horseback –

Prince   The high-speed rider who can shoot a flying
sparrow with his pistol – ?

Falstaff   You've hit it!

Prince   So did he never the sparrow.

Falstaff   Well, that rascal hath good mettle in him, he will
330   not run.

Prince   Why, what a rascal art thou then, to praise him
so for running!

Falstaff   A-horseback, ye cuckoo, but afoot he will not
budge a foot.

335 **Prince**   Yes, Jack, upon instinct.

Falstaff   I grant ye, upon instinct: well, he is there too, and
one Mordake, and a thousand blue-caps more. Worcester
is stolen away tonight; thy father's beard is turned white
with the news; you may buy land now as cheap as stinking
340   mackerel.

Prince   Why then, it is like if there come a hot June, and
this civil buffeting hold, we shall buy maidenheads as they
buy hob-nails, by the hundreds.

Falstaff   By the mass, lad, thou sayest true, it is like we
345   shall have good trading that way. But tell me, Hal, art not
thou horrible afeard? Thou being heir apparent, could the
world pick thee out three such enemies again, as that fiend
Douglas, that spirit Percy, and that devil Glendower? Art
thou not horribly afraid? Doth not thy blood thrill at it?

350 **Prince**   Not a whit, i'faith, I lack some of thy instinct.

Falstaff   Well, thou wilt be horribly chid tomorrow when
thou comest to thy father; if thou love me practise an
answer.

Prince   Do thou stand for my father and examine me upon
355   the particulars of my life.

Falstaff   Shall I? Content! This chair shall be my state, this

Prince He never did the sparrow!

Falstaff Well, he's made of good stuff. He won't run when things get hot.

Prince Why, how rascally of you then, to praise him for covering ground!

Falstaff On horseback, you cuckoo! But on foot, he won't budge a foot.

Prince Except, Jack, upon Instinct . . .

Falstaff I grant you that . . . on Instinct . . . well, he's there, too, and a fellow called Mordake, and a thousand more Scots in blue bonnets. Worcester made off tonight. Your father's beard turned white at the news. You can buy land now as cheap as bad fish.

Prince Well then, come a hot June and the civil war continues, lusty girls will be two a penny.

Falstaff You're right there, lad. We'll strike many a bargain in that direction. But, tell me, Hal: aren't you scared stiff? You being the heir apparent, could you have three worse enemies in all the world than that fiend Douglas, that spirited Percy, and that devil Glendower? Aren't you terrified? Doesn't your blood run cold at it?

Prince Not a bit, I assure you. I lack some of your Instinct . . .

Falstaff Well, you're in for a right old rollicking tomorrow when you visit your father. To please me, practise your reply . . .

Prince Pretend to be my father, and question me about my life-style.

Falstaff Shall I? Great! This chair [*selecting one from a*

119

dagger my sceptre, and this cushion my crown.

Prince   Thy state is taken for a joint-stool, thy golden
sceptre for a leaden dagger, and thy precious rich crown
360   for a pitiful bald crown.

Falstaff   Well, and the fire of grace be not quite out of
thee, now shalt thou be moved. Give me a cup of sack to
make my eyes look red, that it may be thought I have
wept, for I must speak in passion, and I will do it in King
365   Cambyses' vein.

Prince   Well, here is my leg.

Falstaff   And here is my speech. Stand aside, nobility.

Hostess   O Jesu, this is excellent sport, i'faith.

Falstaff   Weep not, sweet Queen, for trickling tears are
370   vain.

Hostess   O the Father, how he holds his countenance!

Falstaff   For God's sake, lords, convey my tristful Queen,
For tears do stop the floodgates of her eyes.

Hostess   O Jesu, he doth it as like one of these harlotry
375   players as ever I see!

Falstaff   Peace, good pint-pot, peace, good tickle-brain.
Harry, I do not only marvel where thou spendest thy
time, but also how thou art accompanied. For though the
camomile, the more it is trodden on the faster it grows,
380   yet youth, the more it is wasted the sooner it wears. That

nearby table] can be my throne, this dagger [*pulling his own from his belt*] can be my sceptre, and this cushion [*finding one handy*] can be my crown.

Prince   Your throne seems to be a stool, your golden sceptre a stage-prop of a dagger, and your precious, priceless crown a pitifully bald one!

Falstaff   Well, provided you aren't totally beyond the pale, you are now going to be deeply moved. Give me a tankard of wine to make my eyes look red, as if I've been crying. I must speak with deep emotion, melodramatically.

Prince   [*bowing*] Well, here's my bended knee.

Falstaff   And here's my speech [*gesturing to his audience*]. Stand to one side, noble people.

Hostess   Oh Jesus! This is great fun, it really is! [*Tears of laughter roll down her face*]

Falstaff   [*in a grand manner*] Weep not, sweet Queen, for trickling tears are vain!

Hostess   Oh God! How does he keep a straight face?

Falstaff   [*with exaggerated gestures*] For God's sake, lords, give succour to my weeping Queen. The floodgates of her eyes are blocked with tears!

Hostess   Oh Jesus! He's as like one of those third-rate repertory players as ever I saw!

Falstaff   Quiet, dear pint-pot; quiet, good head-spinner! [*He clears his throat, then begins with a solemn face and a sober voice*] Harry, I not only wonder about where you spend your time, but also the company you keep. Though camomile flourishes when it is trodden upon, youth (on the other hand) the more it is abused, the quicker it

thou art my son I have partly thy mother's word, partly
my own opinion, but chiefly a villainous trick of thine
eyes, and a foolish hanging of thy nether lip, that doth
warrant me. If then thou be son to me, here lies the
385   point – why, being son to me, art thou so pointed at?
Shall the blessed sun of heaven prove a micher, and eat
blackberries? A question not to be asked. Shall the son of
England prove a thief, and take purses? A question to be
asked. There is a thing, Harry, which thou hast often
390   heard of, and it is known to many in our land by the name
of pitch. This pitch (as ancient writers do report) doth
defile, so doth the company thou keepest: for, Harry, now
I do not speak to thee in drink, but in tears; not in
pleasure, but in passion; not in words only, but in woes
395   also. And yet there is a virtuous man whom I have often
noted in thy company, but I know not his name.

Prince What manner of man, and it like your Majesty?

Falstaff A goodly portly man, i'faith, and a corpulent; of a
cheerful look, a pleasing eye, and a most noble carriage;
400   and, as I think, his age some fifty, or by'r lady inclining to
threescore; and now I remember me, his name is Falstaff.
If that man should be lewdly given, he deceiveth me; for,
Harry, I see virtue in his looks. If then the tree may be
known by the fruit, as the fruit by the tree, then
405   peremptorily I speak it, there is virtue in that Falstaff; him
keep with, the rest banish. And tell me now, thou naughty
varlet, tell me where hast thou been this month?

Prince Dost thou speak like a king? Do thou stand for me,
and I'll play my father.

withers. That you are my son, I have partly your mother's word, and partly my own opinion – but mainly because your eyes look villainous, and your lower lip hangs peculiarly, which is the spit of me. If then you are my son, I'll come to the point: why, being my son, do people point at you so much? Shall the son of God prove to be a truant who went blackberrying? A question not to be asked. Shall the son of the King of England prove to be a thief who steals purses? A question that *must* be asked. There is a certain thing, Harry, which you have often heard of, and which is known to many in our land by the name of 'pitch'. This pitch, as ancient writers have recorded, is prone to defile. So does the company you keep. Harry, I am not speaking to you having had a drop to drink, but having wept tears: not for the pleasure of it, but out of deep emotion. Not just in words, but in woes, too. And yet there is a virtuous man whom I have often noted in your company, but I don't know his name . . .

Prince [*feigning bafflement*] What sort of man, may it please your majesty?

Falstaff A good-looking man of stately bearing, indeed, and well-built. He has a cheerful look, a pleasing eye, and a truly noble deportment. I'd guess his age to be about fifty, or maybe inclining to three score. And now I recall it: his name is Falstaff. If that man should be evilly inclined, he has fooled me. Because Harry, I see virtue in his looks. If 'the tree is known by its fruit', as the fruit is by the tree, then I say this emphatically: there is virtue in that Falstaff. Keep with him. The rest, banish. And now tell me, you naughty boy, where have you been this last month?

Prince [*indicating they should switch roles*] Are you speaking like a King? You stand in for me, and I'll play my father.

410 **Falstaff**   Depose me? If thou dost it half so gravely, so
majestically, both in word and matter, hang me up by the
heels for a rabbit-sucker, or a poulter's hare.

Prince   Well, here I am set.

Falstaff   And here I stand. Judge, my masters.

415 **Prince**   Now, Harry, whence come you?

Falstaff   My noble lord, from Eastcheap.

Prince   The complaints I hear of thee are grievous.

Falstaff   'Sblood, my lord, they are false: nay, I'll tickle ye
for a young prince, i'faith.

420 **Prince**   Swearest thou, ungracious boy? Henceforth ne'er
look on me. Thou art violently carried away from grace,
there is a devil haunts thee in the likeness of an old fat
man, a tun of man is thy companion. Why dost thou con-
verse with that trunk of humours, that bolting-hutch of
425 beastliness, that swollen parcel of dropsies, that huge
bombard of sack, that stuffed cloak-bag of guts, that
roasted Manningtree ox with the pudding in his belly,
that revered vice, that grey iniquity, that father ruffian,
that vanity in years? Wherein is he good, but to taste sack
430 and drink it? wherein neat and cleanly, but to carve a
capon and eat it? wherein cunning, but in craft? wherein

Falstaff   Depose me? If you can do it half so solemnly, so majestically – both in words and gestures – hang me up by the heels like a baby rabbit or a hare in a poulterer's shop!

Prince   [*now seated on the 'throne'*] Well, here I am now seated.

Falstaff   And here I stand. (*To his companions*) Judge, gentlemen.

Prince   (*adopting a heavier voice*) Now, Harry, where have you come from?

Falstaff   (*adopting a lighter one*) My noble lord, from Eastcheap.

Prince   The complaints I've had about you are serious.

Falstaff   Dammit, my lord, they are untrue. (*Everyone roars with laughter. For a brief moment* **Falstaff** *returns to being himself*) I'll give you a young prince that'll tickle you, God knows!

Prince   Did you swear, you profane young man? From now on, don't come near me. You have been violently snatched away from respectability. A devil haunts you in the form of an old, fat man. A human barrel is your companion. Why do you talk to that artery of diseases, that sin-bin of beastliness, that blown-up heap of bodily fluids, that huge magnum of wine, that stuffed suitcase of guts, that roasted ox from Maningtree Fair with stuffing in its belly, that wicked old sinner, that iniquitous greybeard, that elderly hooligan, that reprobate of advanced years! What is he good for but to taste wine and drink it? In what way is he deft and dexterous except in carving a chicken and eating it? In what way is he skilful except in crafty behaviour? In what way clever,

crafty, but in villainy? wherein villainous, but in all
things? wherein worthy, but in nothing?

Falstaff   I would your Grace would take me with you:
435   whom means your Grace?

Prince   That villainous abominable misleader of youth,
Falstaff, that old white-bearded Satan.

Falstaff   My lord, the man I know.

Prince   I know thou dost.

440 **Falstaff**   But to say I know more harm in him than in
myself were to say more than I know. That he is old, the
more the pity, his white hairs do witness it; but that he is,
saving your reference, a whoremaster, that I utterly deny.
If sack and sugar be a fault, God help the wicked! If to be
445   old and merry be a sin, then many an old host that I know
is damned: if to be fat be to be hated, then Pharaoh's lean
kine are to be loved. No, my good lord; banish Peto, banish Bardolph, banish Poins – but for sweet Jack Falstaff,
kind Jack Falstaff, true Jack Falstaff, valiant Jack Falstaff,
450   and therefore more valiant, being as he is old Jack Falstaff,
banish not him thy Harry's company, banish not him thy
Harry's company, banish plump Jack, and banish all the
world.

Prince   I do, I will.

[*A knocking is heard. Exeunt* **Hostess**, **Francis**, *and*
Bardolph]

[*Re-enter* **Bardolph**, *running*]

455 **Bardolph**   O my lord, my lord, the sheriff with a most
monstrous watch is at the door.

except in villainy? In what way villainous, if not in all
things? In what way is he a worthy man? In nothing . . .

Falstaff (*sweetly*) I wish your Grace would explain himself
more clearly. Who does your Grace mean?

Prince That villainous, abominable corrupter of youth,
Falstaff, that old white-bearded Satan.

Falstaff My lord, I know the man.

Prince I know you do.

Falstaff But if I said I knew of more harm in him than in
myself it would be to say more than I know. That he is
old – the more's the pity, and his white hairs bear
witness to it. But that he is, with great respect to you, a
pimp – that I utterly deny. If wine and sugar be a fault,
heaven have mercy on the wicked! If to be old and
cheerful is a sin, then many an old innkeeper I know is
damned. If to be fat means to be hated, then Pharaoh's
lean cows in the Bible are to be loved. No, my good lord:
banish Peto, banish Bardolph, banish Poins. But as for
sweet Jack Falstaff, kind Jack Falstaff, true Jack
Falstaff, valiant Jack Falstaff, (and therefore even more
valiant being, as he is, old Jack Falstaff) – don't banish
him from your son Harry's company; don't banish him
from thy Harry's company. Banish plump Jack, and you
banish all the world!

Prince I do. I will.

[*A knocking is heard at the door. The* **Hostess, Francis**
and **Bardolph** *leave to answer it*]

[**Bardolph** *returns, running*]

Bardolph Oh, my lord, my lord, the sheriff with an awful
lot of constables is at the door!

Falstaff   Out, ye rogue! Play out the play! I have much to say in the behalf of that Falstaff.

[*Re-enter the* **Hostess**]

Hostess   O Jesu, my lord, my lord!

460 **Prince**   Heigh, heigh, the devil rides upon a fiddle-stick, what's the matter?

Hostess   The sheriff and all the watch are at the door; they are come to search the house. Shall I let them in?

Falstaff   Dost thou hear, Hal? Never call a true piece of
465   gold a counterfeit: thou art essentially made without seeming so.

Prince   And thou a natural coward without instinct.

Falstaff   I deny your major. If you will deny the sheriff, so; if not, let him enter. If I become not a cart as well as
470   another man, a plague on my bringing up! I hope I shall as soon be strangled with a halter as another.

Prince   Go hide thee behind the arras, the rest walk up above. Now, my masters, for a true face, and good conscience.

475 **Falstaff**   Both which I have had, but their date is out, and therefore I'll hide me.

[*Exeunt all but the* **Prince** *and* **Peto**]

Prince   Call in the sheriff.

[*Enter* **Sheriff** *and the* **Carrier**]

Falstaff   Be off, you rogue! Finish the play! I have a great deal to say on behalf of that Falstaff.

[*The* **Hostess** *comes back*]

Hostess   Oh Jesus, my lord, my lord!

Prince   We're dancing to the devil's tunes tonight! What's the matter?

Hostess   The sheriff and all the constables are at the door. They've come to search the house. Shall I let them in?

Falstaff   [*worried that the* **Prince** *may denounce him*] Hal, you won't treat a piece of genuine gold like me as if I'm counterfeit? You're the genuine article yourself, though you may not look it . . .

Prince   And you are a natural coward – without Instinct!

Falstaff   A natural coward? I refuse to admit it. If you refuse to admit the sheriff, fine. If not, let him enter. If I don't grace the hangman's cart as much as the next man, be damned to my bringing-up! I trust I'm as good a man as any other to be strangled with a noose.

Prince   Go and hide behind the curtain. The rest of you, go on to the balcony. Now, gentlemen, for an innocent face and a clear conscience.

Falstaff   Both of which I've had, but they are past their best, so therefore I'll hide.

[*Everyone leaves, except the* **Prince** *and* **Peto**]

Prince   Call the sheriff in.

[*Enter the* **Sheriff** *and the* **Porter**]

Now, master sheriff, what is your will with me?

Sheriff First, pardon me, my lord. A hue and cry
480   Hath followed certain men unto this house.

Prince What men?

Sheriff One of them is well known, my gracious lord,
A gross fat man.

Carrier   As fat as butter.

485 **Prince** The man I do assure you is not here,
For I myself at this time have employed him:
And sheriff, I will engage my word to thee,
That I will by tomorrow dinner-time
Send him to answer thee, or any man,
490   For anything he shall be charged withal;
And so let me entreat you leave the house.

Sheriff I will, my lord: there are two gentlemen
Have in this robbery lost three hundred marks.

Prince It may be so: if he have robbed these men
495   He shall be answerable; and so, farewell.

Sheriff Good night, my noble lord.

Prince I think it is good morrow, is it not?

Sheriff Indeed, my lord, I think it be two o'clock.

[*Exit with* **Carrier**]

Prince This oily rascal is known as well as Paul's: go call
500   him forth.

Peto Falstaff! – Fast asleep behind the arras, and snorting
like a horse.

Prince Hark how hard he fetches breath – search his
pockets. What hast thou found?

Now, Master Sheriff, what can I do for you?

Sheriff First, my apologies, my lord. A crowd set up a hue and cry, and followed certain men to this inn.

Prince Which men?

Sheriff One of them is very well known, my gracious lord: a gross, fat man.

Porter As fat as butter!

Prince I can assure you the man is not here: I've given him a job to do for me. You have my guarantee, sheriff, that by dinner-time tomorrow night, I'll send him to account to you or any man for anything that may be charged against him. So, may I ask you to leave this house?

Sheriff I will, my lord, Two gentlemen have lost £200 in this robbery.

Prince It may well be so. If he has robbed these men, he shall be answerable. So – goodbye. [*He shows them the door*]

Sheriff Good night, my noble lord.

Prince I think it's 'good morning', isn't it?

Sheriff Indeed, my lord – I think it's 2 a.m.

[*He leaves with the* **Porter**]

Prince This fat rascal is as well known as St Paul's Cathedral. Go and bring him out.

Peto [*shouting*] Falstaff! [*He takes a closer look*] Fast asleep behind the curtain, and snoring like a horse!

Prince Listen how he snores! Search his pockets. [**Peto** *does so*] What have you found?

505 **Peto**   Nothing but papers, my lord.

Prince   Let's see what they be, read them.

Peto	Item a capon	2s	2d
	Item sauce		4d
	Item sack two gallons	5s	8d
510	Item anchovies and sack		
	after supper	2s	6d
	Item bread		$\frac{1}{2}$d

Prince   O monstrous! but one halfpennyworth of bread to
this intolerable deal of sack? What there is else keep close,
515   we'll read it at more advantage. There let him sleep till
day; I'll to the court in the morning. We must all to the
wars, and thy place shall be honourable. I'll procure this
fat rogue a charge of foot, and I know his death will be a
march of twelve score. The money shall be paid back
520   again with advantage. Be with me betimes in the morning;
and so, good morrow, Peto.

Peto   Good morrow, good my lord.

[*Exeunt*]

Peto   Nothing but papers, my lord.

Prince   Let's see what they are. Read them!

Peto   [*reading*]

Item: one chicken	12	pence
Item: sauce	2	pence
Item: wine, two gallons	28	pence
Item: anchovies and wine after supper	$12\frac{1}{2}$	pence
Item: bread	$\frac{1}{2}$	pence

Prince   How outrageous! Only one halfpenny's worth of bread to this incredible amount of wine? Whatever else there is, keep hidden; we'll read it at a more convenient time. He can sleep there till daylight. I'll go to Court in the morning. We must all be off to the wars – I'll see you have a good commission. I'll get a troop of infantry for this fat rogue: he won't survive a march of two hundred and forty paces! The money shall be repaid with interest. Join me early in the morning. So – good morning, Peto.

Peto   [*bowing*] Good morning, good my lord.

[*They leave*]

Act three

Scene 1

Bangor. The Archdeacon's House. Enter **Hotspur,
Worcester, Lord Mortimer, Owen Glendower**

Mortimer   These promises are fair, the parties sure,
And our induction full of prosperous hope.

Hotspur   Lord Mortimer, and cousin Glendower, will you
   sit down?
And uncle Worcester. A plague upon it!
I have forgot the map.

Glendower   No, here it is:
Sit, cousin Percy, sit, good cousin Hotspur;
For by that name as oft as Lancaster doth speak of you
His cheek looks pale, and with a rising sigh
He wisheth you in heaven.

Hotspur   And you in hell,
As oft he hears Owen Glendower spoke of.

Glendower   I cannot blame him; at my nativity
The front of heaven was full of fiery shapes,
Of burning cressets, and at my birth
The frame and huge foundation of the earth
Shaked like a coward.

Hotspur   Why, so it would have done
At the same season if your mother's cat
Had but kittened, though yourself had never been born.

Glendower   I say the earth did shake when I was born.

134

Act three

Scene 1

Owen Glendower's Castle, North Wales. **Hotspur, Worcester, Lord Mortimer,** *and* **Owen Glendower** *are conferring*

Mortimer [*indicating documents*] These are fair promises. Our allies are reliable. This is an auspicious beginning.

Hotspur Lord Mortimer, and cousin Glendower: do sit down – and Uncle Worcester. Dammit, I've forgotten the map.

Glendower No – here it is. [*To* **Hotspur**] Sit, cousin Percy; sit, good cousin Hotspur. Whenever Lord John of Lancaster refers to you by that name, his cheeks pale: and with an expressive sigh he wishes you in heaven.

Hotspur And you in hell, whenever he hears the name Owen Glendower!

Glendower I can't blame him. At my birth, the sky was filled with the fiery shapes of burning beacons, and the world's huge mass quaked with fear.

Hotspur Well, so it would have done at that time of the year if your mother's cat had just had kittens, and you had never been born.

Glendower [*emphatically*] I tell you the earth shook when I was born!

Hotspur   And I say the earth was not of my mind,
20   If you suppose as fearing you it shook.

Glendower   The heavens were all on fire, the earth did
      tremble –

Hotspur   O, then the earth shook to see the heavens on
      fire,
      And not in fear of your nativity.
      Diseased nature oftentimes breaks forth
25   In strange eruptions; oft the teeming earth
      Is with a kind of colic pinched and vexed
      By the imprisoning of unruly wind
      Within her womb, which for enlargement striving
      Shakes the old beldam earth, and topples down
30   Steeples and moss-grown towers. At your birth
      Our grandam earth, having this distemp'rature,
      In passion shook.

Glendower   Cousin, of many men
      I do not bear these crossings; give me leave
35   To tell you once again that at my birth
      The front of heaven was full of fiery shapes,
      The goats ran from the mountains, and the herds
      Were strangely clamorous to the frighted fields.
      These signs have marked me extraordinary,
      And all the courses of my life do show
40   I am not in the roll of common men.
      Where is he living, clipped in with the sea
      That chides the banks of England, Scotland, Wales,
      Which calls me pupil or hath read to me?
      And bring him out that is but woman's son
45   Can trace me in the tedious ways of art,
      And hold me pace in deep experiments.

Hotspur   I think there's no man speaks better Welsh:
      I'll to dinner.

Hotspur   And I say the earth thought differently from me, if you reckon it shook because you frightened it.

Glendower   [*getting angry*] The heavens were all on fire, and the earth trembled!

Hotspur   Well, then, the earth shook when it saw the heavens on fire, and not because of your birth. When nature's sick, it frequently breaks out in strange eruptions. Often the fertile earth is cramped and troubled with a sort of colic, caused by the trapping of troublesome wind inside her womb. When this seeks relief, old grandmother earth rumbles, causing church steeples and moss covered towers to topple down. When you were born, our granny earth shook violently through belching.

Glendower   [*trying to control himself*] Cousin, not many men would I allow to cross me like this. Give me leave to tell you once again that at my birth the sky was full of fiery shapes. Goats ran from the mountains. Herds stamped the frightened fields most strangely. These signs have marked me out as different, and all the events in my life have shown that I'm no ordinary man. Is there a man alive, living within the sea-boundaries of England, Scotland or Wales, who can claim to be my master, or to have taught me anything? Show me any mortal woman's son who can follow my tracks in the subtleties of magic, or keep abreast of me in profound experiments.

Hotspur   [*contemptuously, mocking **Glendower's** accent*] I think there's no one who speaks better Welsh. [*Turning away*] I'm going to dinner.

Mortimer   Peace, cousin Percy, you will make him mad.

50 **Glendower**   I can call spirits from the vasty deep.

Hotspur   Why, so can I, or so can any man.
But will they come when you do call for them?

Glendower   Why, I can teach you, cousin, to command the
devil.

Hotspur   And I can teach thee, coz, to shame the devil
55   By telling truth; tell truth, and shame the devil.
If thou have power to raise him, bring him hither,
And I'll be sworn I have power to shame him hence:
O, while you live, tell truth, and shame the devil!

Mortimer   Come, come, no more of this unprofitable chat.

60 **Glendower**   Three times hath Henry Bolingbroke made
head
Against my power, thrice from the banks of Wye
And sandy-bottomed Severn have I sent him
Bootless home, and weather-beaten back.

Hotspur   Home without boots, and in foul weather too!
65   How scapes he agues, in the devil's name?

Glendower   Come, here is the map, shall we divide our
right
According to our threefold order ta'en?

Mortimer   The Archdeacon hath divided it
70   Into three limits very equally;
England, from Trent and Severn hitherto,
By south and east is to my part assigned:
All westward, Wales beyond the Severn shore,
And all the fertile land within that bound,

Mortimer   Quiet, cousin Percy! You'll annoy him!

Glendower   [*insisting, and holding* **Hotspur** *back*] I can summon up spirits from the depths of the earth!

Hotspur   Why, so can I, or so can anyone. But will they come when you send for them?

Glendower   Why, I can teach you, cousin, to give orders to the devil!

Hotspur   And I can teach you, friend, to shame the devil – by telling the truth. 'Tell truth, and shame the devil'. If you have the gift of summoning him, bring him here: I'll swear I've got the power to shame him away. Oh, while you have living breath, tell the truth and shame the devil!

Mortimer   [*uneasy*] Come, come. No more of this pointless chat.

Glendower   [*glaring, but deciding to start the meeting*] Three times Henry Bolingbroke has advanced against my armies. Three times from the banks of the River Wye, and the sandy-bottomed River Severn, I've sent him home defeated, beaten back by the inclement weather.

Hotspur   [*whispering and mocking unmercifully*] De-feeted? Home without boots, and in foul weather, too! How did he escape catching cold, in the devil's name?

Glendower   Come. Here's the map. Shall we divide our shares according to our triple alliance?

Mortimer   The Archdeacon has divided it into three regions, very equally. England, stretching from the river Trent eastwards and the River Severn southwards, is allotted to me. All to the west – Wales beyond the shores of the Severn, and all the fertile land within that

To Owen Glendower: and, dear coz, to you
75 The remnant northward lying off from Trent.
And our indentures tripartite are drawn,
Which being sealed interchangeably,
(A business that this night may execute)
Tomorrow, cousin Percy, you and I
80 And my good Lord of Worcester will set forth
To meet your father and the Scottish power,
As is appointed us, at Shrewsbury.
My father Glendower is not ready yet,
Nor shall we need his help these fourteen days.
85 [*To* **Glendower**] Within that space you may have drawn
together
Your tenants, friends, and neighbouring gentlemen.

Glendower A shorter time shall send me to you, lords,
And in my conduct shall your ladies come,
90 From whom you now must steal and take no leave,
For there will be a world of water shed
Upon the parting of your wives and you.

Hotspur Methinks my moiety, north from Burton here,
In quantity equals not one of yours:
See how this river comes me cranking in,
95 And cuts me from the best of all my land
A huge half-moon, a monstrous cantle out.
I'll have the current in this place dammed up,
And here the smug and silver Trent shall run
In a new channel fair and evenly;
100 It shall not wind with such a deep indent,
To rob me of so rich a bottom here.

Glendower Not wind? It shall, it must – you see it doth.

Mortimer Yea,
But mark how he bears his course, and runs me up
105 With like advantage on the other side,

boundary — is Owen Glendower's; and to you, [*addressing* **Hotspur**] dear cousin, the remaining territory lying north of the Trent. Our three-way contracts have been drawn up; once we've signed all three, something we can do tonight, then tomorrow, Cousin Percy, you and I will set forth to meet your father and the Scottish troops which have been assigned to us, at Shrewsbury. My father-in-law Glendower isn't ready yet, nor shall we need his help for at least a fortnight. [*To* **Glendower**] By that time you can bring together your tenants, friends, and neighbouring gentlemen.

Glendower   I'll be with you sooner, my lords, and I'll bring your ladies with me. You must sneak away without saying farewell, otherwise there'll be an ocean of tears shed at your departure from them.

Hotspur   [*scanning the map in close detail*] I think my share, north from the town of Burton here, is not as large as either of yours. See how this river [*pointing*] comes curving in, and cuts a half-moon off the best of all my land. A huge lump out! I'll have the river dammed up here, so the smooth and silver Trent will flow along a new bed, fairly and evenly. I won't have it winding with such a deep indentation, robbing me of such a rich river valley.

Glendower   Not wind? It shall — it must — you see it does!

Mortimer   Yes, [*to* **Hotspur**, *persuasively*] but notice how it keeps its course, and affords me a similar disadvantage

Gelding the opposed continent as much
As on the other side it takes from you.

Worcester   Yea, but a little charge will trench him here,
And on this north side win this cape of land,
110   And then he runs straight and even.

Hotspur   I'll have it so, a little charge will do it.

Glendower   I'll not have it altered.

Hotspur
                          Will not you?

Glendower   No, nor you shall not.

Hotspur
                          Who shall say me
nay?

Glendower   Why, that will I.

115 **Hotspur**   Let me not understand you then, speak it in
       Welsh.

Glendower   I can speak English, lord, as well as you,
For I was trained up in the English court,
Where being but young I framed to the harp
Many an English ditty lovely well,
120   And gave the tongue a helpful ornament –
A virtue that was never seen in you.

Hotspur   Marry and I am glad of it with all my heart!
I had rather be a kitten and cry 'mew'
Than one of these same metre ballad-mongers;
125   I had rather hear a brazen canstick turned,
Or a dry wheel grate on the axle-tree,
And that would set my teeth nothing on edge,
Nothing so much as mincing poetry –
'Tis like the forced gait of a shuffling nag.

130 **Glendower**   Come, you shall have Trent turned.

on the other side: cutting as much from the opposite bank as it does from yours.

Worcester Yes, but a bit of gunpowder will dam it here, and on this north side regain this stretch of land. Then it will run straight and even.

Hotspur That's what I want. A small charge will do it.

Glendower I'll not have it altered.

Hotspur Oh, really?

Glendower No, you won't!

Hotspur And who'll stop me?

Glendower I will!

Hotspur [*with sweeping gesture of contempt*] Let's say I didn't hear that. Say it in Welsh . . .

Glendower [*eyes blazing*] I can speak English, lord, as well as you. I was brought up in the English court, where when I was very young I transcribed for the harp many an English song extremely well, and added attractive words to the music – something you've never done!

Hotspur And I'm indeed very glad of it! I'd rather be a kitten, crying 'miaou!' than one of these cheap penny-poets! I'd rather hear a brass candlestick being turned on a lathe, or an unlubricated wheel scrape on its axle stub. Neither of these would set my teeth on edge half so much as pansy poetry; it's like the unwilling trot of a clapped-out nag!

Glendower [*seeing he cannot win*] All right. You shall have the river Trent's course changed.

Hotspur   I do not care, I'll give thrice so much land
To any well-deserving friend:
But in the way of bargain, mark ye me,
I'll cavil on the ninth part of a hair.
135   Are the indentures drawn? Shall we be gone?

Glendower   The moon shines fair, you may away by night:
I'll haste the writer, and withal
Break with your wives of your departure hence.
I am afraid my daughter will run mad,
140   So much she doteth on her Mortimer.

[*Exit*]

Mortimer   Fie, cousin Percy, how you cross my father!

Hotspur   I cannot choose; sometimes he angers me
With telling me of the moldwarp and the ant,
Of the dreamer Merlin and his prophecies,
145   And of a dragon and a finless fish,
A clip-winged griffin and a moulten raven,
A couching lion and a ramping cat,
And such a deal of skimble-skamble stuff
As puts me from my faith. I tell you what –
150   He held me last night at least nine hours
In reckoning up the several devils' names
That were his lackeys: I cried 'Hum', and 'Well, go to!'
But marked him not a word. O, he is as tedious
As a tired horse, a railing wife,
155   Worse than a smoky house. I had rather live
With cheese and garlic in a windmill, far,
Than feed on cates and have him talk to me
In any summer house in Christendom.

Mortimer   In faith, he is a worthy gentleman,
160   Exceedingly well read, and profited
In strange concealments, valiant as a lion,

Hotspur [*having won, now indifferent to the victory*] I
don't care. I'd give three times as much land to a well-
deserving friend. But by way of a bargain, mark my word,
I'll argue over one-ninth of a single hair. Are the
contracts ready? Shall we be off?

Glendower   The moon is bright. You can leave tonight. I'll
make the clerk hurry up. Tell your wives of your
departure from here. I'm afraid my daughter will be most
distressed; she dotes on her Mortimer so much.

[*He leaves*]

Mortimer   For shame, cousin Percy. How you do cross my
father-in-law!

Hotspur   I can't help it. Sometimes he angers me with his
stories of the mole and the ant, of the prophetic Merlin,
of the dragon and a finless fish, a clipped-winged Griffin
and a moulting raven, a lion 'couchant' and a cat
'rampant' – enough meaningless legendary rubbish to
put me off religion. I tell you what, he cornered me for
fully nine hours last night while he reckoned up the
names of the various devils who were his servants. I
cried 'Ahem!' and 'Well, how amazing!' but I took no
notice of what he said. Oh, he's as boring as a weary
horse, a shrewish wife, and far worse than a smoky
house. I'd much rather live on cheese and onions in a
windmill, than feed on cakes and dainties and have him
talk to me in any summer house in Christendom!

Mortimer   Really, he's a very upright gentleman:
exceedingly well-read, expert in the secret arts, valiant
as a lion, amazingly good-tempered, and as generous as

And wondrous affable, and as bountiful
As mines of India. Shall I tell you, cousin?
He holds your temper in a high respect
165 And curbs himself even of his natural scope
When you come 'cross his humour, faith he does:
I warrant you that man is not alive
Might so have tempted him as you have done
Without the taste of danger and reproof:
170 But do not use it oft, let me entreat you.

Worcester   In faith, my lord, you are too wilful-blame,
And since your coming hither have done enough
To put him quite besides his patience;
You must needs learn, lord, to amend this fault.
175 Though sometimes it show greatness, courage, blood,
– And that's the dearest grace it renders you –
Yet oftentimes it doth present harsh rage,
Defect of manners, want of government,
Pride, haughtiness, opinion, and disdain,
180 The least of which haunting a nobleman
Loseth men's hearts and leaves behind a stain
Upon the beauty of all parts besides,
Beguiling them of commendation.

Hotspur   Well, I am schooled – good manners be your
185   speed!
Here come our wives, and let us take our leave.

[*Enter* **Glendower** *with the* **Ladies**]

Mortimer   This is the deadly spite that angers me,
My wife can speak no English, I no Welsh.

Glendower   My daughter weeps, she'll not part with you,
She'll be a soldier too, she'll to the wars.

the mines of India. Shall I tell you what, cousin? He has a
great respect for your temper, and controls his natural
impulses when you clash with him temperamentally.
Really he does. I assure you that there isn't a living man
who could have provoked him as you have done without
risking danger and rebuke. But don't do it too often, I beg
of you.

Worcester Really, my lord, you are too headstrong. Since
you came here, you've done more than enough to try his
patience. You must learn to control this fault. Though it
sometimes indicates greatness, courage, spirit – and in
you these are nobly present – on the other hand, it
sometimes suggests rude anger, bad manners, lack of
self-control, pride, haughtiness, arrogance and
contempt. A nobleman afflicted by the least of these
loses men's loyalty. His finer qualities are blotted out:
denied their recognition.

Hotspur Well, I stand corrected. [*Sardonically*] May good
manners bring you success! Here come our wives, so
let's say our farewells.

[*Enter* **Glendower** *and the* **Ladies**]

Mortimer This is my great affliction: my wife speaks no
English, and I no Welsh . . .

Glendower My daughter is crying! She'll not part with you.
She wants to be a soldier too, and go to war.

147

190 **Mortimer**   Good father, tell her that she and my aunt
Percy
Shall follow in your conduct speedily.

[**Glendower** *speaks to her in Welsh, and she answers him in
the same.*]

Glendower   She is desperate here, a peevish, self-willed
harlotry, one that no persuasion can do good upon.

[*The* **Lady** *speaks in Welsh*]

Mortimer   I understand thy looks; that pretty Welsh
195   Which thou pourest down from these swelling heavens
I am too perfect in, and but for shame
In such a parley should I answer thee.

[*The* **Lady** *speaks again in Welsh*]

I understand thy kisses, and thou mine,
200   And that's a feeling disputation,
But I will never be a truant, love,
Till I have learnt thy language, for thy tongue
Makes Welsh as sweet as ditties highly penned,
Sung by a fair queen in a summer's bow'r
With ravishing division to her lute.

205 **Glendower**   Nay, if you melt, then will she run mad.

[*The* **Lady** *speaks again in Welsh*]

Mortimer   O, I am ignorance itself in this!

Glendower   She bids you on the wanton rushes lay you
down,
And rest your gentle head upon her lap,

Mortimer Father dear, tell her that she and my Aunt Percy
will follow in your company very quickly.

[**Glendower** *speaks to her in Welsh, and she replies in the
same*]

Glendower She's in despair: a peevish, self-willed little
wench, who can't be persuaded.

[*The* **Lady** *speaks in Welsh again*]

Mortimer I understand your looks, and those pretty Welsh
tears leave me in no doubt. Shame prevents me from
replying in the same tearful idiom.

[*The* **Lady** *speaks again in Welsh*]

I understand your kisses, and you mine, and they
communicate most touchingly. I shall never truant again
from school till I have learned to speak your language.
Your voice makes Welsh as sweet as flowery ballads
sung by a beautiful queen in a summery glade, most
lyrically, to the accompaniment of her lute.

Glendower If it melted your heart, she would go mad!

[*The* **Lady** *again speaks in Welsh*]

Mortimer [*straining to understand, but failing to*] I am all
ignorance!

Glendower [*translating*] She asks you to lie down on the
comfortable rush-mats, and to rest your gentle head

And she will sing the song that pleaseth you,
210 And on your eyelids crown the god of sleep,
Charming your blood with pleasing heaviness,
Making such difference 'twixt wake and sleep
As is the difference betwixt day and night,
The hour before the heavenly-harnessed team
215 Begins his golden progress in the east.

Mortimer   With all my heart I'll sit and hear her sing,
By that time will our book I think be drawn.

Glendower   Do so, and those musicians that shall play to
you
Hang in the air a thousand leagues from hence,
220 And straight they shall be here: sit, and attend.

Hotspur   Come, Kate, thou art perfect in lying down:
Come, quick, quick, that I may lay my head in thy lap.

Lady Percy   Go, ye giddy goose.

[*The music plays*]

Hotspur   Now I perceive the devil understands Welsh,
225 And 'tis no marvel he is so humorous,
By'r lady, he is a good musician.

Lady Percy   Then should you be nothing but musical,
For you are altogether governed by humours.
Lie still, ye thief, and hear the lady sing in Welsh.

230 **Hotspur**   I had rather hear Lady my brach howl in Irish.

Lady Percy   Would'st thou have thy head broken?

Hotspur   No.

Lady Percy   Then be still.

Hotspur   Neither, 'tis a woman's fault.

upon her lap. She will sing your favourite song and, your eyelids closed in sleep, she'll make you feel a pleasant drowsiness: the sort of twilight zone between wakefulness and sleep that's like the hour between daytime and night.

Mortimer   I'll sit here with all my heart, and listen to her sing. By that time, our agreement will, I think, be drawn up.

Glendower   Do: and the musicians who will play to you are hovering in the air a thousand miles from here. [*The magician speaks now*] They'll be here at once. Sit down, and listen.

Hotspur   [*suggestively, mocking the lovers' interlude*] Come, Kate . . . you're good at lying down . . . Come! quick, quick . . . so that I can lay my head in your lap . . .

Lady Percy   [*blushing*] Go away, you silly goose!

Hotspur   Now I realize the devil can understand Welsh, I'm not surprised he's so temperamental. [*The music begins*] My word, he's a great musician!

Lady Percy   In that case, you should be musical through and through. You are all temperament! [*Poking him*] Lie still, you thief, and listen to the lady sing in Welsh!

Hotspur   I'd rather hear Lady, my bitch-hound, howl in Irish!

Lady Percy   Do you want your head broken?

Hotspur   No . . .

Lady Percy   Then lie still!

Hotspur   Not that either! That's for women . . .

151

235 **Lady Percy**   Now God help thee!

Hotspur   To the Welsh lady's bed.

Lady Percy   What's that?

Hotspur   Peace, she sings. Come, Kate, I'll have your song too.

Lady Percy   Not mine, in good sooth.

240 **Hotspur**   Not yours, in good sooth! Heart, you swear like a comfit-maker's wife – 'Not you, in good sooth!', and 'As true as I live!', and 'As God shall mend me!', and 'As sure as day!' –
And givest such sarcenet surety for thy oaths
As if thou never walk'st further than Finsbury.
245 Swear me, Kate, like a lady as thou art,
A good mouth-filling oath, and leave 'In sooth',
And such protest of pepper-gingerbread,
To velvet-guards, and Sunday citizens.
Come, sing.

250 **Lady Percy**   I will not sing.

Hotspur   'Tis the next way to turn tailor, or be redbreast teacher. And the indentures be drawn I'll away within these two hours; and so come in when ye will.

[*Exit*]

255 **Glendower**   Come, come, Lord Mortimer, you are as slow
As hot Lord Percy is on fire to go:
By this our book is drawn – we'll but seal,
And then to horse immediately.

Lady Percy   [*covering his offending lips, and blushing*] God help you!

Hotspur   [*incorrigible, pulling her hand away*] To get into the Welsh lady's bed . . . ?

Lady Percy   [*a warning finger raised*] What's that you said?

Hotspur   Sh! She's singing . . . [*The* **Lady** *sings a Welsh song*] Come on, Kate. Let's have your song too!

Lady Percy   Not mine, for heaven's sake.

Hotspur   Not yours, for heaven's sake! Dear heart, you swear like a cachou-maker's wife [*Copying her voice*] 'Not you, for heaven's sake!' and 'As true as I'm standing here!' and 'God forgive me!' and 'As sure as day!' Your oaths have such a pure-silk softness about them, you'd think you'd never been out in the real world! Like the aristocrat you are, Kate, swear good mouth-filling oaths! Leave 'for heaven's sake' and other such prissy exclamations to the stuffed shirts, the Sunday-best brigade. Come on, sing!

Lady Percy   [*emphatically*] I will not sing!

Hotspur   You'll never be a tailor, then, or train songbirds! [*Rising to his feet, businesslike now. To* **Glendower**] Once the agreement is drawn up, I'll be away in under two hours. Call me when you are ready.

[*He leaves abruptly*]

Glendower   [*drawing his son-in-law away*] Come, come, Lord Mortimer. You are as slow to leave as the hot-blooded Lord Percy is on fire to go. Our contract will have been prepared by now. We'll just stop to sign, then take to our horses immediately.

Mortimer   With all my heart.

                                              [*Exeunt*]

Scene 2

London. The Palace. Enter the **King**, **Prince of Wales**, *and others.*

King   Lords, give us leave; the Prince of Wales and I
        Must have some private conference: but be near at hand,
        For we shall presently have need of you.

                                         [*Exeunt* **Lords**]

        I know not whether God will have it so
5   For some displeasing service I have done,
        That in his secret doom out of my blood
        He'll breed revengement and a scourge for me;
        But thou dost in thy passages of life
        Make me believe that thou art only marked
10   For the hot vengeance and the rod of heaven,
        To punish my mistreadings. Tell me else
        Could such inordinate and low desires,
        Such poor, such bare, such lewd, such mean attempts,
        Such barren pleasures, rude society,
15   As thou art matched withal, and grafted to,
        Accompany the greatness of thy blood,
        And hold their level with thy princely heart?

    Prince   So please your Majesty, I would I could
        Quit all offences with as clear excuse

Mortimer   [*a soldier again*] With all my heart!

[*They leave*]

Scene 2

The Palace in London. Enter the **King**, *the* **Prince of Wales**,
Lords *and* **Attendants**.

King   My lords: leave us now. The Prince of Wales and I
wish to talk privately together. Don't go far. We shall
need you again shortly.

[*The* **Lords** *and* **Attendants** *leave*]

[*To the* **Prince**] Perhaps, because of something I've done
wrong, God has ordained that my own flesh and blood
should punish me. Your life-style makes me think that
heaven is working out its fierce revenge through you.
How else could such unbecoming and low tastes – such
contemptible, such wretched, such base, such mean
pursuits, such mindless pleasures and uncouth
companions as you associate with and seem so attached
to – possibly co-exist with the greatness of your
breeding, or match your princely rank?

Prince   With respect to your majesty, I wish I could clear
myself of all offences as simply and convincingly as I'm

20 As well as I am doubtless I can purge
   Myself of many I am charged withal:
   Yet such extenuation let me beg
   As, in reproof of many tales devised,
   Which oft the ear of greatness needs must hear,
. 25 By smiling pickthanks, and base newsmongers,
   I may for some things true, wherein my youth
   Hath faulty wandered and irregular,
   Find pardon on my true submission.

  King God pardon thee! Yet let me wonder, Harry,
30 At thy affections, which do hold a wing
   Quite from the flight of all thy ancestors.
   Thy place in Council thou hast rudely lost,
   Which by thy younger brother is supplied,
   And art almost an alien to the hearts
35 Of all the court and princes of my blood:
   The hope and expectation of thy time
   Is ruined, and the soul of every man
   Prophetically do forethink thy fall.
   Had I so lavish of my presence been,
40 So common-hackneyed in the eyes of men,
   So stale and cheap to vulgar company,
   Opinion, that did help me to the crown,
   Had still kept loyal to possession,
   And left me in reputeless banishment,
45 A fellow of no mark nor likelihood.
   By being seldom seen, I could not stir
   But like a comet I was wondered at,
   That men would tell their children, 'This is he!'
   Others would say, 'Where, which is Bolingbroke?'
50 And then I stole all courtesy from heaven,
   And dressed myself in such humility
   That I did pluck allegiance from men's hearts,
   Loud shouts and salutations from their mouths,
   Even in the presence of the crowned King.

sure I can discharge myself of many I'm accused of now.
Let me beg this favour: that in return for disproving many
of the fictions that must reach your ear via fawning
favour-seekers and shabby rumour-mongers, I may be
forgiven some of the true faults I've committed in my
wayward youth.

King   God forgive you! But let me express surprise, Harry,
at your tastes. They are quite at odds with those of all
your ancestors. You have lost your membership of the
Council through boorishness, to be replaced by your
younger brother, and you have almost alienated yourself
from the affections of the entire court and the royal
family. The hopes and expectations of your future reign
lie in ruins. Everyone, deep down, predicts you are in
for a fall. If I had been so generous with my personal
appearances, so well-known to the public, so over-
exposed and accessible to the lower classes, public
opinion (which helped me to the throne) would have
stayed loyal to Richard, and I would have remained in
obscure banishment, an undistinguished fellow without
prospects. By being rarely seen, I could not leave the
house without being the centre of curious attention, like
a comet. Men would say to their children 'This is him!'
Others would say 'Where? Which is this Bolingbroke?'
Whereupon I assumed a godlike graciousness, and
affected such humility that I stole the hearts of men,
eliciting loud approving shouts and greetings, even when
in the presence of the rightful King. That way I kept

55   Thus did I keep my person fresh and new,
      My presence, like a robe pontifical,
      Ne'er seen but wondered at; and so my state,
      Seldom, but sumptuous, showed like a feast,
      And won by rareness such solemnity.
60   The skipping King, he ambled up and down,
      With shallow jesters, and rash bavin wits,
      Soon kindled and soon burnt; carded his state,
      Mingled his royalty with cap'ring fools;
      Had his great name profaned with their scorns,
65   And gave his countenance against his name
      To laugh at gibing boys, and stand the push
      Of every beardless vain comparative;
      Grew a companion to the common streets,
      Enfeoffed himself to popularity,
70   That, being daily swallowed by men's eyes,
      They surfeited with honey, and began
      To loathe the taste of sweetness, whereof a little
      More than a little is by much too much.
      So, when he had occasion to be seen,
75   He was but as the cuckoo is in June,
      Heard, not regarded; seen, but with such eyes
      As, sick and blunted with community,
      Afford no extraordinary gaze,
      Such as is bent on sun-like majesty
80   When it shines seldom in admiring eyes;
      But rather drowsed and hung their eyelids down,
      Slept in his face, and rendered such aspect
      As cloudy men use to their adversaries,
      Being with his presence glutted, gorged, and full.
85   And in that very line, Harry, standest thou,
      For thou hast lost thy princely privilege
      With vile participation. Not an eye
      But is a-weary of thy common sight,
      Save mine, which hath desired to see thee more,

myself always fresh and new. Like a bishop's robe my
appearance was always a matter for amazement. Thus,
my presence, infrequent but spectacular, was like a
feast, all the more impressive for its rarity. Richard, the
lightweight king, mingled with superficial jesters, and
those flashy wits who are quick to be sparked off but
soon extinguished. He cheapened himself, rubbing his
royal shoulders with frolicking fools; suffering his royal
title to be demeaned by their scornfulness; good-
humouredly tolerating the jibes of upstarts, in a most
unkingly fashion; putting up with the cheek of every
young pipsqueak. He frequented the public streets, and
surrendered himself to low company. So that, being on
daily view, men saw too much of him, and reacted
against him. Too much of a good thing makes it quite
unpalatable. When he had a real reason for being seen,
he was rather like a cuckoo in June – heard, but not
regarded; seen, but with eyes so blinkered with
familiarity that they showed no special reaction, as they
should when gazing upon the kind of sun-like majesty
that shines very rarely upon admiring eyes. On the
contrary, they looked drowsy, hooded, asleep even,
giving an appearance rather like sullen men facing their
enemies – being so satiated by his presence. That's
precisely, Harry, where you stand. You've lost your royal
authority through mixing with low companions. Everyone
is weary of the sight of you except me, who'd like to see

90   Which now doth that I would not have it do,
        Make blind itself with foolish tenderness.

Prince   I shall hereafter, my thrice gracious lord,
        Be more myself.

King   For all the world
        As thou art to this hour was Richard then
95   When I from France set foot at Ravenspurgh,
        And even as I was then is Percy now.
        Now by my sceptre, and my soul to boot,
        He hath more worthy interest to the state
        Than thou the shadow of succession.
100   For of no right, nor colour like to right,
        He doth fill fields with harness in the realm,
        Turns head against the lion's armed jaws,
        And being no more in debt to years than thou
        Leads ancient lords and reverend bishops on
105   To bloody battles, and to bruising arms.
        What never-dying honour hath he got
        Against renowned Douglas! whose high deeds,
        Whose hot incursions and great name in arms,
        Holds from all soldiers chief majority
110   And military title capital
        Through all the kingdoms that acknowledge Christ.
        Thrice hath this Hotspur, Mars in swathling clothes,
        This infant warrior, in his enterprises
        Discomfited great Douglas, ta'en him once,
115   Enlarged him, and made a friend of him,
        To fill the mouth of deep defiance up,
        And shake the peace and safety of our throne.
        And what say you to this? Percy, Northumberland,
        The Archbishop's Grace of York, Douglas, Mortimer,
120   Capitulate against us and are up.
        But wherefore do I tell these news to thee?
        Why, Harry, do I tell thee of my foes,

you more. And now, in spite of myself, my eyes are blind
with foolish, tender tears. [*He weeps*]

Prince   [*kneeling*] From now on, my most gracious lord, I
shall behave more properly.

King   You are for all the world like Richard was when I
landed at Ravenspurgh from France. And just as I was
then, so Harry Percy is right now. By my sceptre and my
very soul: he can claim the throne through merit; you are
just my heir! Without a case, or anything resembling a
case, he leads armies to the field, and fearlessly
challenges the mighty. No older than yourself, he leads
elderly lords and reverend bishops into bloody battles and
engagements. What undying honour he earned against
the famous Douglas, whose great exploits, heroic
invasions and great military reputation make him first and
foremost amongst soldiers throughout Christendom!
Three times this Hotspur – this god of war new-born,
this infant warrior – has got the better of mighty
Douglas. He captured him once, then let him go –
making him a friend to add to the chorus of defiant
voices that shake the peace and safety of our throne.
What do you say to this? Harry Percy, Northumberland,
His Grace the Archbishop of York, Douglas, and
Mortimer unite against us and are mobilized. But why do I
tell this news to you? Why, Harry, do I tell you about my

Which art my nearest and dearest enemy?
Thou that art like enough, through vassal fear,
125 Base inclination, and the start of spleen,
To fight against me under Percy's pay,
To dog his heels, and curtsy at his frowns,
To show how much thou art degenerate.

Prince   Do not think so, you shall not find it so;
130 And God forgive them that so much have swayed
Your Majesty's good thoughts away from me!
I will redeem all this on Percy's head,
And in the closing of some glorious day
Be bold to tell you that I am your son,
135 When I will wear a garment all of blood,
And stain my favours in a bloody mask,
Which, washed away, shall scour my shame with it;
And that shall be the day, whene'er it lights,
That this same child of honour and renown,
140 This gallant Hotspur, this all-praised knight,
And your unthought-of Harry chance to meet.
For every honour sitting on his helm,
Would they were multitudes, and on my head
My shames redoubled! For the time will come
145 That I shall make this northern youth exchange
His glorious deeds for my indignities.
Percy is but my factor, good my lord,
To engross up glorious deeds on my behalf,
And I will call him to so strict account
150 That he shall render every glory up,
Yea, even the slightest worship of his time,
Or I will tear the reckoning from his heart.
This in the name of God I promise here,
The which if He be pleased I shall perform,
155 I do beseech your Majesty may salve
The long-grown wounds of my intemperance:
If not, the end of life cancels all bands,

foes, when you're my nearest and my dearest enemy?
You, who as like as not through cowardly fear, mischief,
and sheer spite will fight against me in Percy's pay,
following at his heels and fawning when he frowns, to
show how low you've fallen!

Prince   You mustn't think that! That's not how it is! And
God forgive those who have so prejudiced your Majesty
against me! I'll put everything to rights by defecting
Percy, and at the end of a glorious day's battle
sometime, I'll make bold to claim that I'm your son. I'll be
soaked in blood, my face a bloody mask; when I wash it
clean, all my shame will be cleansed away. That will be
the day, come when it will – when this so-called 'child of
honour and renown', this gallant Hotspur, this knight so
universally praised, chances to meet with your low-rated
Harry. I wish his honours could be multiplied, and my
shames doubled! Because the time will surely come
when I'll make this northern youngster exchange his glorious deeds for my shortcomings. Percy is acting as my
agent, good my lord. He's piling up glorious deeds on my
behalf! But I'll be so tough with him, he'll have to
surrender his triumphs – yes, even the smallest of them!
– or I'll have his heart instead. This I pledge here in God's
name. If it's His will that I succeed, I hope your Majesty
will find it heals the longstanding wounds of my
licentious living. If it's not, then death cancels all debts.

And I will die a hundred thousand deaths
Ere break the smallest parcel of this vow.

160 **King**   A hundred thousand rebels die in this –
Thou shalt have charge and sovereign trust herein.

[*Enter* **Blunt**]

How now, good Blunt? Thy looks are full of speed.

Blunt   So hath the business that I come to speak of.
Lord Mortimer of Scotland hath sent word
165 That Douglas and the English rebels met
The eleventh of this month at Shrewsbury.
A mighty and a fearful head they are,
If promises be kept on every hand,
As ever offered foul play in a state.

170 **King**   The Earl of Westmoreland set forth today,
With him my son, Lord John of Lancaster,
For this advertisement is five days old.
On Wednesday next, Harry, you shall set forward,
On Thursday we ourselves will march.
175 Our meeting is Bridgnorth, and, Harry, you
Shall march through Gloucestershire, by which account,
Our business valued, some twelve days hence
Our general forces at Bridgnorth shall meet.
Our hands are full of business, let's away,
180 Advantage feeds him fat while men delay.

[*Exeunt*]

I'd die a hundred thousand times before I'd break the smallest fraction of this vow.

King   In saying that, a hundred thousand rebels died! You shall be given responsibility and absolute trust in these matters!

[**Sir Walter Blunt** *enters*]

Well now, good Blunt? There's an urgent look about you . . .

Blunt   So too is the business I've come about. Lord Mortimer of Scotland has sent word that Douglas and the English rebels met at Shrewsbury on the eleventh of this month. If they all stick together, they're as mighty and powerful a force as ever got up to dirty work against the state.

King   This news is five days old. The Earl of Westmoreland left today with my son, Lord John of Lancaster. Next Wednesday, Harry, you must set off. On Thursday, I myself will march. Bridgnorth is our meeting place, and, Harry, you must march through Gloucestershire: which, all things considered, should bring us all together at Bridgnorth twelve days from now. We've a lot to do. Let's go. Delay is dangerous.

[*They leave*]

Scene 3

Eastcheap. The Boar's Head Tavern. Enter **Falstaff** *and*
Bardolph

Falstaff   Bardolph, am I not fallen away vilely since this
last action? Do I not bate? Do I not dwindle? Why, my
skin hangs about me like an old lady's loose gown. I am
withered like an old apple-john. Well, I'll repent, and that
5   suddenly, while I am in some liking; I shall be out of heart
shortly, and then I shall have no strength to repent. And I
have not forgotten what the inside of a church is made of,
I am a peppercorn, a brewer's horse: the inside of a
church! Company, villainous company, hath been the
10   spoil of me.

Bardolph   Sir John, you are so fretful you cannot live long.

Falstaff   Why, there is it: come, sing me a bawdy song,
make me merry. I was as virtuously given as a gentleman
need to be; virtuous enough; swore little; diced not above
15   seven times – a week; went to a bawdy-house not above
once in a quarter – of an hour; paid money that I borrowed – three or four times; lived well, and in good compass; and now I live out of all order, out of all compass.

Bardolph   Why, you are so fat, Sir John, that you must
20   needs be out of all compass, out of all reasonable compass,
Sir John.

Falstaff   Do thou amend thy face, and I'll amend my life:
thou art our admiral, thou bearest the lantern in the poop,
but 'tis in the nose of thee: thou art the Knight of the
25   Burning Lamp.

Scene 3

The tavern at Eastcheap. Enter **Falstaff** *and* **Bardolph**

Falstaff Bardolph, haven't I wasted away dreadfully since our last action, at Gad's Hill? Haven't I lost weight? Aren't I fading away? My skin's hanging off me like an old woman's dressing gown! I'm withered like a rotten apple. Well, I'll repent, and soon too, while there's still something of me left. I'll be out of condition shortly, and then I won't have the strength to repent. If I haven't forgotten what the inside of a church looks like, I'm a dried old peppercorn or a knackered old nag. The inside of a church? [*He shakes his head gravely*] Company – villainous companions! – have been the ruin of me!

Bardolph Sir John, you're fretting away so much, you won't live much longer . . .

Falstaff Well, there it is! Come on, sing me a smutty song! Cheer me up! I used to be as virtuously inclined as a gentleman ought to be. I was virtuous enough. I swore very little, gambled not more than seven times a week, went to a brothel not more than once every fifteen minutes, repaid my debts on three or four occasions, lived well, and under control. Now I live all out of order. Out of all control . . .

Bardolph Why, you're so fat, Sir John, you've got to be out of all control – out of all reasonable control, Sir John.

Falstaff [*eyeing* **Bardolph's** *carbuncles and boils*] You get your face fixed, and I'll sort out my life . . . . You are our pilot-ship with the flashing light at the back. Only in your case it's at the front: your nose. You are the Knight of the Flashing Lantern.

167

Bardolph   Why, Sir John, my face does you no harm.

Falstaff   No, I'll be sworn, I make as good use of it as
many a man doth of a death's-head, or a *memento mori*. I
never see thy face but I think upon hell-fire, and Dives
30   that lived in purple: for there he is in his robes, burning,
burning. If thou wert any way given to virtue, I would
swear by thy face: my oath should be 'By this fire, that's
God's angel!' But thou art altogether given over; and wert
indeed, but for the light in thy face, the son of utter dark-
35   ness. When thou ran'st up Gad's Hill in the night to catch
my horse, if I did not think thou hadst been an *ignis
fatuus*, or a ball of wildfire, there's no purchase in money.
O, thou art a perpetual triumph, an everlasting
bonfirelight! Thou hast saved me a thousand marks in
40   links and torches, walking with thee in the night betwixt
tavern and tavern: but the sack that thou hast drunk me
would have bought me lights as good cheap at the dearest
chandler's in Europe. I have maintained that salamander
of yours with fire any time this two and thirty years, God
45   reward me for it!

Bardolph   'Sblood, I would my face were in your belly!

Falstaff   God-a-mercy! so should I be sure to be
heartburnt.

[*Enter* **Hostess**]

How now, Dame Parlet the hen, have you enquired yet
50   who picked my pocket?

Hostess   Why, Sir John, what do you think, Sir John, do
you think I keep thieves in my house? I have searched, I
have enquired, so has my husband, man by man, boy by
boy, servant by servant – the tithe of a hair was never lost
55   in my house before.

Bardolph   My face does you no harm, Sir John!

Falstaff   No, indeed! I make as good a use of it as many a
man does of a death's head or a 'memento mori'. I never
look at your face without thinking of hell-fire, and rich old
misers like Dives in the Bible: there he is in his posh
clothes, burning, burning. If you were in the slightest bit
virtuous, I'd swear by your face: I'd say 'By this fire, it's
the angel of God!' But you're altogether corrupted. But
for the light in your face, you'd be a son of outer
darkness. When you ran up Gad's Hill during the night to
catch my horse, if I didn't take you for a will-o-the-wisp
or a firework, cash isn't currency any more. Oh, you're a
perpetual torch, an everlasting bonfire-light! You've
saved me a thousand pounds in flares and torches, walking between taverns at night – but the wine you've drunk
at my expense would have bought me lights just as
cheaply at the dearest candlemaker's in Europe! I've
provided that dragon of yours with its fire these thirty-
two years, God reward me for it!

Bardolph   I wish my face was in your guts!

Falstaff   Merciful heavens! You'd give me heart-burn!

[*Enter the* **Hostess**, *fussily*]

Hello, Dame Clutterbuck! Have you found out who
picked my pocket yet?

Hostess   Why, Sir John, what do you mean, Sir John? Do
you think I keep thieves in my house? I've searched, I've
enquired; so has my husband – man by man, boy by boy,
servant by servant. Not so much as the tenth part of a
hair has gone missing in my house before.

Falstaff   Ye lie, hostess: Bardolph was shaved and lost
many a hair, and I'll be sworn my pocket was picked: go
to, you are a woman, go.

Hostess   Who, I? No, I defy thee: God's light, I was never
60   called so in mine own house before.

Falstaff   Go to, I know you well enough.

Hostess   No, Sir John, you do not know me, Sir John, I
know you, Sir John, you owe me money, Sir John, and
now you pick a quarrel to beguile me of it. I bought you a
65   dozen of shirts to your back.

Falstaff   Dowlas, filthy dowlas. I have given them away to
bakers' wives; they have made bolters of them.

Hostess   Now as I am a true woman, holland of eight
shilling an ell! You owe money here besides, Sir John, for
70   your diet, and by-drinkings, and money lent you, four and
twenty pound.

Falstaff   He had his part of it, let him pay.

Hostess   He? Alas, he is poor, he hath nothing.

Falstaff   How? Poor? Look upon his face. What call you
75   rich? Let them coin his nose, let them coin his cheeks, I'll
not pay a denier. What, will you make a younker of me?
Shall I not take mine ease in mine inn but I shall have my
pocket picked? I have lost a seal-ring of my grandfather's
worth forty mark.

80   **Hostess**   O Jesu, I have heard the Prince tell him, I know
not how oft, that that ring was copper.

Falstaff   How? the Prince is a Jack, a sneak-up. 'Sblood,
and he were here I would cudgel him like a dog if he
would say so.

170

Falstaff That's a lie, hostess! Bardolph's been shaved here and lost many a hair. And I'll swear my pocket was picked! Be off with you! You're no lady! Go!

Hostess Who, me? By God, I was never called that in my house before!

Falstaff Get away! I know you well enough!

Hostess Oh no, Sir John, you don't know me, Sir John. I know you, Sir John. You owe me money, Sir John. Now you're picking a quarrel to cheat me out of it. I bought you a dozen shirts to wear.

Falstaff Hessian – lousy hessian! I gave them away to bakers' wives for sifting flour!

Hostess Now as I'm a decent woman, they were fine linen at eight pounds a yard. And you owe money here besides, Sir John, for food and drinks-between-meals, and for money loaned to you. Two hundred and forty pounds!

Falstaff [*indicating* **Baldolph**] He had his share. He can pay.

Hostess Him? Alas, he's poor. He's got nothing.

Falstaff What? Poor? Look at his face. Isn't that rich? They could mint his nose. Coin his cheeks. I won't pay a brass farthing. Do you think I'm a greenhorn? Can't I sit at my ease in my own inn without having my pocket picked? I've lost a signet-ring of my grandfather's worth thirty pounds.

Hostess Oh Jesus! I've heard the Prince tell him a thousand times that that ring was made of copper!

Falstaff What? The Prince is a rascal! A sneak! Hell's bells, if he were here now, I'd beat him like a dog if he said that . . . . [*He picks up a stick and wafts it around*]

171

[*Enter the* **Prince** *marching, with* **Peto,** *and* **Falstaff** *meets him, playing upon his truncheon like a fife*]

85   How now, lad? Is the wind in that door, i'faith, must we all march?

Bardolph   Yea, two and two, Newgate fashion.

Hostess   My lord, I pray you hear me.

Prince   What say'st thou, Mistress Quickly? How doth thy
90   husband? I love him well, he is an honest man.

Hostess   Good my lord, hear me.

Falstaff   Prithee let her alone, and list to me.

Prince   What say'st thou, Jack?

Falstaff   The other night I fell asleep here, behind the
95   arras, and had my pocket picked: this house is turned bawdy-house, they pick pockets.

Prince   What didst thou lose, Jack?

Falstaff   Wilt thou believe me, Hal, three or four bonds of forty pound apiece, and a seal-ring of my grandfather's.

100 **Prince**   A trifle, some eightpenny matter.

Hostess   So I told him, my lord, and I said I heard your Grace say so: and, my lord, he speaks most vilely of you, like a foul-mouthed man as he is, and said he would cudgel you.

105 **Prince**   What! he did not?

Hostess   There's neither faith, truth, nor womanhood in me else.

[*The* **Prince** *and* **Poins** *enter, marching in military fashion.*
Falstaff *turns the stick into an imaginary fife, and meets
them in the same style*]

Well now, lad! Is that the way the wind's blowing? Are
we on the march?

Bardolph   Yes – two by two. Ark fashion.

Hostess   My lord, could I have a word?

Prince   Yes, Mrs Quickly? How's your husband? I like him a
lot. He's a good man.

Hostess   Good my lord, it's like this . . .

Falstaff   Let her be, and listen to me!

Prince   You were saying, Jack?

Falstaff   The other night I fell asleep here behind the
curtain and had my pocket picked. This inn's turning into
a brothel. They pick your pockets.

Prince   What did you lose, Jack?

Falstaff   Would you believe it, Hal? Three or four bonds
worth four hundred pounds each, and a signet ring of my
grandfather's.

Prince   A mere nothing. Rubbish.

Hostess   So I told him, my lord, and I said I heard Your
Grace say so too. And, my lord, he speaks very vilely
about you, like the foul-mouthed man he is. He said he'd
beat you.

Prince   What? He didn't!

Hostess   There's neither faith, truth or womanhood in me
otherwise.

173

Falstaff   There's no more faith in thee than in a stewed
prune, nor no more truth in thee than in a drawn
110   fox – and for womanhood, Maid Marian may be the depu-
ty's wife of the ward to thee. Go, you thing, go!

Hostess   Say, what thing, what thing?

Falstaff   What thing? Why, a thing to thank God on.

Hostess   I am no thing to thank God on, I would thou
115   shouldst know it, I am an honest man's wife, and setting
thy knighthood aside, thou art a knave to call me so.

Falstaff   Setting thy womanhood aside, thou art a beast to
say otherwise.

Hostess   Say, what beast, thou knave, thou?

120   **Falstaff**   What beast? Why, an otter.

Prince   An otter, Sir John? Why an otter?

Falstaff   Why? She's neither fish nor flesh, a man knows
not where to have her.

Hostess   Thou art an unjust man in saying so, thou or any
125   man knows where to have me, thou knave, thou.

Prince   Thou say'st true, hostess, and he slanders thee most
grossly.

Hostess   So he doth you, my lord, and said this other day
you ought him a thousand pound.

130   **Prince**   Sirrah, do I owe you a thousand pound?

Falstaff   A thousand pound, Hal? A million, thy love is
worth a million, thou owest me thy love.

Hostess   Nay, my lord, he called you Jack, and said he
would cudgel you.

135   **Falstaff**   Did I, Bardolph?

Falstaff There's no more faith in you than in a whore. No more truth in you than a hunted fox. And as for womanhood, the town harlot's a vicar's wife compared with you. Get away! You thing, you!

Hostess What thing? Go on – what thing?

Falstaff What thing? A thing to thank God for!

Hostess [*shocked*] I'm not a thing to thank God for, I'll have you know! I'm an honest man's wife. Your knighthood to one side, you're a rascal to call me that!

Falstaff Setting your womanhood to one side, you're a beast to deny it.

Hostess What beast, you rascal, you?

Falstaff What beast? Why, an otter!

Prince An otter, Sir John? Why an otter?

Falstaff Why? Because she's neither fish nor flesh. A man wouldn't know how to take her!

Hostess You are an unjust man to say that. You or any man knows where to take me, you rascal you!

Prince That's true, hostess, and he is slandering you most improperly . . .

Hostess And he did you, too, my lord. The other day he said you owed him a thousand pounds.

Prince Hey – do I owe you a thousand pounds?

Falstaff A thousand pounds, Hal? A million! Your love is worth a million. You owe me your love . . .

Hostess No, my lord. He called you a rascal, and said he'd beat you.

Falstaff Did I, Bardolph?

175

Bardolph   Indeed, Sir John, you said so.

Falstaff   Yea, if he said my ring was copper.

Prince   I say 'tis copper, darest thou be as good as thy word now?

140 **Falstaff**   Why, Hal, thou knowest as thou art but man I dare, but as thou art prince, I fear thee as I fear the roaring of the lion's whelp.

Prince   And why not as the lion?

Falstaff   The King himself is to be feared as the lion: dost
145   thou think I'll fear thee as I fear thy father? Nay, and I do, I pray God my girdle break.

Prince   O, if it should, how would thy guts fall about thy knees! But sirrah, there's no room for faith, truth, nor honesty in this bosom of thine; it is all filled up with guts
150   and midriff. Charge an honest woman with picking thy pocket? Why, thou whoreson impudent embossed rascal, if there were anything in thy pocket but tavern reckonings, memorandums of bawdy-houses, and one poor pennyworth of sugar-candy to make thee long-winded, if thy
155   pocket were enriched with any other injuries but these, I am a villain: and yet you will stand to it, you will not pocket up wrong! Art thou not ashamed?

Falstaff   Dost thou hear, Hal? Thou knowest in the state of innocency Adam fell, and what should poor Jack Falstaff
160   do in the days of villainy? Thou seest I have more flesh than another man, and therefore more frailty. You confess then, you picked my pocket?

Prince   It appears so by the story.

Falstaff   Hostess, I forgive thee, go make ready breakfast,
165   love thy husband, look to thy servants, cherish thy guests,

Bardolph   Indeed, Sir John, you did.

Falstaff   Yes – if he said my ring was made of copper!

Prince   I say it *is* copper. Dare you be as good as your word now?

Falstaff   Why, Hal, you know that as you are a mere man, I dare. But as you are a prince, I fear you as I fear the offspring of a lion.

Prince   Why not as the lion?

Falstaff   The King himself is to be feared as the lion. Do you think I'll fear you as I fear your father? No. If I did – pray God my belt should break!

Prince   If it did, your guts would fall down to your knees! In that bosom of yours there's no room for faith, truth or honesty. It's all filled up with guts and midriff. Charge an honest woman with picking your pocket? Why, you foul, impudent, swollen rascal! If there was anything in your pocket but tavern bills, notes on brothels, and a mere pennyworth of barley-sugar to give you energy – if your pockets were enriched with any other losses than these – I'm a villain! Yet you'll stand there telling lies! Exposing your wickedness! Aren't you ashamed?

Falstaff   Listen, Hal. You know Adam fell from grace when in a state of innocence. So what chance does poor Jack Falstaff stand in days of villainy? You can see I've more flesh than other men, therefore I have more frailty. You admit, then, that you picked my pocket?

Prince   It would appear so . . .

Falstaff   Hostess: I forgive you. Go and get breakfast ready. Love your husband. Look after the servants.

thou shalt find me tractable to any honest reason, thou
seest I am pacified still, nay prithee be gone.

[*Exit* **Hostess**]

Now, Hal, to the news at court: for the robbery, lad, how
is that answered?

170 **Prince** O my sweet beef, I must still be good angel to
thee – the money is paid back again.

Falstaff O, I do not like that paying back, 'tis a double
labour.

Prince I am good friends with my father and may do
175 anything.

Falstaff Rob me the exchequer the first thing thou dost,
and do it with unwashed hands too.

Bardolph Do, my lord.

Prince I have procured thee, Jack, a charge of foot.

180 **Falstaff** I would it had been of horse. Where shall I find
one that can steal well? O for a fine thief of the age of two
and twenty or thereabouts: I am heinously unprovided.
Well, God be thanked for these rebels, they offend none
but the virtuous; I laud them, I praise them.

185 **Prince** Bardolph!

Bardolph My lord?

Prince Go bear this letter to Lord John of Lancaster,
To my brother John, this to my Lord of Westmoreland.

[*Exit* **Bardolph**]

Go, Peto, to horse, to horse, for thou and I

Cherish your guests. You'll find me a very reasonable man. I'm easily satisfied, as you can see. [*The* **Hostess** *is about to make a retort, but he raises his hand to stop her*] No, off you go! [*The* **Hostess** *gives up and leaves*] Now, Hal – to turn to court matters. About the robbery, lad. What's the situation?

Prince   Well, my old beefsteak, I've still got to be your guardian angel. The money has been paid back again.

Falstaff   Oh, I don't like the sound of that 'paying back'! It's twice the work!

Prince   I've made it up with my father, and I can do anything now.

Falstaff   Rob the Exchequer for starters. Don't hesitate!

Bardolph   Yes, do, my lord.

Prince   I've got a commission for you, Jack; an infantry brigade.

Falstaff   I'd have preferred cavalry. Where can I recruit a good thief? Oh for a good thief . . . aged twenty-two, or thereabouts . . . I'm desperately underprovided. Well, thank God for these rebels. Only the virtuous are offended by them. I honour them. I praise them.

Prince   Bardolph!

Bardolph   My lord?

Prince   Take this letter to Lord John of Lancaster – my brother John. And this one to my Lord of Westmoreland. [**Bardolph** *goes*] Peto – see to the horses. You and I have

179

190   Have thirty miles to ride yet ere dinner-time.

                                        [*Exit* **Peto**]

       Jack, meet me tomorrow in the Temple-hall
       At two o'clock in the afternoon:
       There shalt thou know thy charge, and there receive
       Money and order for their furniture.
195   The land is burning, Percy stands on high,
       And either we or they must lower lie.

                                        [*Exit*]

   Falstaff   Rare words! Brave world! Hostess, my breakfast,
       come!
       O, I could wish this tavern were my drum.

                                        [*Exit*]

thirty miles to ride by dinner-time. [**Peto** *exits*] Jack, meet me tomorrow afternoon in Temple Hall, at two o'clock. I'll tell you your regiment, and give you money and an indent for their equipment. The country is ablaze. Percy rides high. They, or we, must fall.

[*They go*]

Falstaff   Fine words! Brave world! Hostess, bring my breakfast! Oh, I wish this tavern could be my rallying-point.

Act four

Scene 1

Shrewsbury. The Rebel Camp. Enter **Hotspur**, **Worcester**, *and* **Douglas**

Hotspur   Well said, my noble Scot! If speaking truth
In this fine age were not thought flattery,
Such attribution should the Douglas have
As not a soldier of this season's stamp
5   Should go so general current through the world.
By God, I cannot flatter, I do defy
The tongues of soothers, but a braver place
In my heart's love hath no man than yourself:
Nay, task me to my word, approve me, lord.

10 **Douglas**   Thou art the king of honour:
No man so potent breathes upon the ground
But I will beard him.

Hotspur   Do so, and 'tis well.

[*Enter a* **Messenger** *with letters*]

What letters has thou there? – I can but thank you.

Messenger   These letters come from your father.

15 **Hotspur**   Letters from him? Why comes he not himself?

Messenger   He cannot come, my lord, he is grievous sick.

Hotspur   'Zounds, how has he the leisure to be sick
In such a justling time? Who leads his power?
Under whose government come they along?

Act four

Scene 1

The rebel camp near Shrewsbury. Enter **Hotspur,**
Douglas, *and* **Worcester.**

Hotspur   [*to* **Douglas**] Well said, my noble Scot! If speaking
the truth weren't thought of as flattery these days, no
top-class soldier anywhere would more deserve my
compliments than you. By God, I can't flatter – I despise
sweet talk – but no man has a more respected place in
my heart than you. Put me to the proof: try me out . . .

Douglas   You are the king of honour. I'll tackle any man, no
matter who he is.

Hotspur   Do that: that's right. [*A* **Messenger** *arrives.*
Hotspur *reaches out his hand*] What letters have you
there? [*To* **Douglas** *again*] I can only thank you.

Messenger   Letters from your father.

Hotspur   Letters from him? Why doesn't he come himself?

Messenger   He can't come, my lord. He's very sick.

Hotspur   God's truth, how can he find time to be sick at
such a critical time? Who's in charge of his army? Under
whose command are they coming?

20 **Messenger**   His letters bear his mind, not I, my lord.

Worcester   I prithee tell me, doth he keep his bed?

Messenger   He did, my lord, four days ere I set forth,
      And at the time of my departure thence
      He was much feared by his physicians.

25 **Worcester**   I would the state of time had first been whole
      Ere he by sickness had been visited:
      His health was never better worth than now.

Hotspur   Sick now? Droop now? This sickness doth infect
      The very life-blood of our enterprise;
30   'Tis catching hither, even to our camp.
      He writes me here that inward sickness –
      And that his friends by deputation could not
      So soon be drawn, nor did he think it meet
      To lay so dangerous and dear a trust
35   On any soul removed but on his own.
      Yet doth he give us bold advertisement
      That with our small conjunction we should on,
      To see how fortune is disposed to us;
      For, as he writes, there is no quailing now,
40   Because the King is certainly possessed
      Of all our purposes. What say you to it?

Worcester   Your father's sickness is a maim to us.

Hotspur   A perilous gash, a very limb lopped off –
      And yet, in faith, it is not! His present want
45   Seems more than we shall find it. Were it good
      To set the exact wealth of all our states
      All at one cast? to set so rich a main
      On the nice hazard of one doubtful hour?
      It were not good, for therein should we read
50   The very bottom and the soul of hope,
      The very list, the very utmost bound
      Of all our fortunes.

Messenger   His letters convey his plans, my lord, not I.

Worcester   Tell me, has he taken to his bed?

Messenger   Yes, my lord; four days before I left. His doctors were very worried about him as I departed.

Worcester   I wish things had been sorted out first, before he went sick. Never was his good health more needed than now.

Hotspur   Sick now? Flagging now? This sickness infects the very life-blood of our venture. The disease is spreading, as far as our own camp. [*He scans the letter*] He writes here that some internal sickness . . . [*He reads the details to himself, then turns the page over and speaks again*] . . . and that his friends wouldn't rally round anyone deputizing for him. Nor did he think it right to delegate a dangerous and important matter to anyone less personally concerned than himself. Yet he strongly advises us to press on with our small alliance, to see how things go; because – so he writes – there's no flinching now. The King certainly knows all our plans. [*He looks up*] What do you say to that?

Worcester   Your father's sickness is a great handicap to us.

Hotspur   A dangerous wound – like having a limb chopped off! And yet, though, it isn't! We're exaggerating his importance. Would it be sensible to venture our all on one throw of the dice? To stake so much on the risky gamble of one unpredictable engagement? No, it wouldn't! Because if we did, we'd be speculating all our hopes and expectations and defining their utmost limits!

Douglas   Faith, and so we should, where now remains
A sweet reversion – we may boldly spend
55   Upon the hope of what is to come in.
A comfort of retirement lives in this.

Hotspur   A rendezvous, a home to fly unto,
If that the devil and mischance look big
Upon the maidenhead of our affairs.

60 **Worcester**   But yet I would your father had been here:
The quality and hair of our attempt
Brooks no division; it will be thought,
By some that know not why he is away,
That wisdom, loyalty, and mere dislike
65   Of our proceedings kept the Earl from hence;
And think how such an apprehension
May turn the tide of fearful faction,
And breed a kind of question in our cause:
For well you know we of the off'ring side
70   Must keep aloof from strict arbitrement,
And stop all sight-holes, every loop from whence
The eye of reason may pry in upon us:
This absence of your father's draws a curtain
That shows the ignorant a kind of fear
75   Before not dreamt of.

Hotspur   You strain too far.
I rather of his absence make this use:
It lends a lustre and more great opinion,
A larger dare to our great enterprise,
Than if the Earl were here; for men must think
80   If we without his help can make a head
To push against a kingdom, with his help
We shall o'erturn it topsy-turvy down.
Yet all goes well, yet all our joints are whole.

Douglas   As heart can think: there is not such a word
85   Spoke of in Scotland as this term of fear.

Douglas   Indeed, so we would! We have the prospect of a future windfall; we can spend confidently now on the expectation of what's to come. We've got resources to fall back upon . . .

Hotspur   . . . a bolthole, a refuge to escape to, if things go badly for us . . .

Worcester   Nevertheless, I wish your father could be here. Ours is the kind of scheme that needs a united front. People who don't know why he's missing will think that cautiousness, loyalty, and sheer dislike of our methods have kept the Earl away. Consider how such thoughts might turn the tide with our wavering supporters, and raise an element of doubt about our cause. You well know that we, the challengers, must avoid being examined too carefully, and must present a blank front to those with prying eyes. This absence of your father's exposes certain dangers which the uninformed had never feared before.

Hotspur   You're worrying too much. I'd take his absence this way: it makes our great venture more illustrious, more prestigious, more daring, than if the Earl were here. Men will think that if we can make headway and put pressure on the establishment, then with his help we'll turn it upside down. All's still going well. We're still in one piece.

Douglas   Wholeheartedly. There's no such word as 'fear' in Scotland!

[*Enter* **Sir Richard Vernon**]

Hotspur   My cousin Vernon! Welcome, by my soul!

Vernon   Pray God my news be worth a welcome, lord.
The Earl of Westmoreland seven thousand strong
Is marching hitherwards, with him Prince John.

90 **Hotspur**   No harm, what more?

Vernon   And further, I have learned,
The King himself in person is set forth,
Or hitherwards intended speedily,
With strong and mighty preparation.

95 **Hotspur**   He shall be welcome too: where is his son,
The nimble-footed madcap Prince of Wales,
And his comrades that daft the world aside
And bid it pass?

Vernon   All furnished, all in arms;
All plumed like estridges that with the wind
100 Bated, like eagles having lately bathed,
Glittering in golden coats like images,
As full of spirit as the month of May,
And gorgeous as the sun at midsummer;
Wanton as youthful goats, wild as young bulls.
I saw young Harry with his beaver on,
105 His cushes on his thighs, gallantly armed,
Rise from the ground like feathered Mercury,
And vaulted with such ease into his seat
As if an angel dropped down from the clouds
To turn and wind a fiery Pegasus,
110 And witch the world with noble horsemanship.

[*Enter* **Sir Richard Vernon**]

Hotspur   Cousin Vernon! Welcome, upon my soul!

Vernon   Please God my news is worth a welcome, lord.
The Earl of Westmoreland, with seven thousand men, is
marching towards us. Prince John is with him.

Hotspur   That's all right. What else?

Vernon   I've also learned that the King himself has set out.
He's also making for here at full speed with a large army.

Hotspur   He'll be welcome, too. Where's his son – the
dashing, tearaway Prince of Wales – and his comrades,
who've dropped out of society?

Vernon   They're all fully equipped, all mobilized, all adorned
like ostriches, their crests fluttering in the wind like
eagles beating wings after bathing; their gilded coats of
mail glittering like painted statues. They're as sprightly
as the month of May, as gorgeous as the sun at
midsummer, as giddy as youthful goats; as wild as young
bulls. I saw young Prince Harry – helmeted, armour
round his thighs, valiantly armed – rise from the ground
like the winged god Mercury, and vault into the saddle
with such ease it was as if an angel dropped down from
the clouds to handle skilfully a fiery steed, entrancing the
world with noble horsemanship.

Hotspur   No more, no more! Worse than the sun in
    March,
    This praise doth nourish agues. Let them come!
    They come like sacrifices in their trim,
    And to the fire-eyed maid of smoky war
115   All hot and bleeding will we offer them:
    The mailed Mars shall on his altar sit
    Up to the ears in blood. I am on fire
    To hear this rich reprisal is so nigh,
    And yet not ours! Come, let me taste my horse,
120   Who is to bear me like a thunderbolt
    Against the bosom of the Prince of Wales.
    Harry to Harry shall, hot horse to horse,
    Meet and ne'er part till one drop down a corse.
    O that Glendower were come!

125 **Vernon**   There is more news:
    I learned in Worcester as I rode along
    He cannot draw his power this fourteen days.

Douglas   That's the worst tidings that I heard of yet.

Worcester   Ay, by my faith, that bears a frosty sound.

Hotspur   What may the King's whole battle reach unto?

130 **Vernon**   To thirty thousand.

Hotspur
                               Forty let it be:
    My father and Glendower being both away,
    The powers of us may serve so great a day.
    Come, let us take a muster speedily –
    Doomsday is near; die all, die merrily.

135 **Douglas**   Talk not of dying, I am out of fear
    Of death or death's hand for this one half year.

                                                    [*Exeunt*]

190

Hotspur   All right, all right. This praise gives me the shudders more than sunshine in early spring. Let 'em come! They come like beasts to the slaughter. We'll offer them, all hot and bleeding, as sacrifices to the war goddess, Bellona; and the war god Mars shall sit up to his ears in blood upon his throne. It rouses me to hear so rich a prize is near at hand, and not yet ours! Come, then. Let me sample my horse, which is going to charge like a thunderbolt towards the Prince of Wales. Harry shall fight Harry, gallant horse against horse: meeting but not parting till one drops down dead! I wish Glendower were here . . .

Vernon   There's more news. On my way I learned in Worcester that he can't muster his troops for at least a fortnight.

Douglas   That's the worst news yet!

Worcester   Yes, indeed. That's cold comfort.

Hotspur   How many men has the King?

Vernon   About thirty thousand.

Hotspur   So what if it's forty? Our armies can cope perfectly well even without my father and Glendower! Let's rally the troops immediately. Doomsday is near. Roll on death!

Douglas   Don't talk about death. Death and dying don't scare me right now!

[*They go*]

191

Scene 2

A public road near Coventry. Enter **Falstaff** *and* **Bardolph**

Falstaff   Bardolph, get thee before to Coventry; fill me a
bottle of sack. Our soldiers shall march through; we'll to
Sutton Co'fil' tonight.

Bardolph   Will you give me money, captain?

5 **Falstaff**   Lay out, lay out.

Bardolph   This bottle makes an angel.

Falstaff   And if it do, take it for thy labour – and if it make
twenty, take them all, I'll answer the coinage. Bid my
lieutenant Peto meet me at town's end.

10 **Bardolph**   I will, captain: farewell.

[*Exit*]

Falstaff   If I be not ashamed of my soldiers, I am a soused
gurnet; I have misused the King's press damnably. I have
got in exchange of a hundred and fifty soldiers three
15   hundred and odd pounds. I press me none but good
householders, yeoman's sons, inquire me out contracted
bachelors, such as had been asked twice on the banns,
such a commodity of warm slaves as had as lief hear the
devil as a drum, such as fear the report of a caliver worse
than a struck fowl or a hurt wild duck. I pressed me none
20   but such toasts-and-butter, with hearts in their bellies no
bigger than pins' heads, and they have bought out their
services; and now my whole charge consists of ancients,
corporals, lieutenants, gentlemen of companies – slaves
as ragged as Lazarus in the painted cloth, where the
25   glutton's dogs licked his sores: and such as indeed were

Scene 2

A highway near Coventry. Enter **Falstaff** *and* **Bardolph**. *A ragged regiment stands at a distance.*

Falstaff   Bardolph, you go on ahead to Coventry. Get me some wine. We'll march straight through and aim for Sutton Coldfield tonight.

Bardolph   Can I have some money, captain?

Falstaff   Put it on the bill.

Bardolph   [*writing it down*] Another bottle makes [*He does some quick arithmetic*] ten pounds.

Falstaff   Well, if it does, keep it for making it. Even if it makes twenty, keep the lot. I'll take the responsibility. Tell Lieutenant Peto to meet me outside the town.

Bardolph   I will, captain. [*He salutes*] Farewell.

Falstaff   If I'm not ashamed of my soldiers, call me a pickled herring! I've abused my commission damnably. In exchange for the hundred and fifty soldiers I've pressed into service, I've got over three hundred pounds. I only conscript solid citizens, the sons of the comfortably-off. I look for men about to be married, whose banns have been called twice. The kind of well-heeled ninnies who'd rather hear the devil than a military drum. The sort who fear a rifle shot more than the cry of a wounded woodcock or a winged wild duck! I conscripted milksops like these with hearts inside 'em the size of pinheads. They've bought their discharges. Now my whole brigade consists of standard-bearers, corporals, lieutenants, NCO's: wretches as ragged as Lazarus in the wall-pictures that show his sores being licked by the glutton

never soldiers, but discarded unjust servingmen, younger
sons to younger brothers, revolted tapsters, and ostlers
trade-fallen, the cankers of a calm world and a long peace,
ten times more dishonourable-ragged than an old fazed
30   ancient; and such have I to fill up the rooms of them as
have bought out their services, that you would think that I
had a hundred and fifty tattered prodigals lately come
from swine-keeping, from eating draff and husks. A mad
fellow met me on the way, and told me I had unloaded all
35   the gibbets and pressed the dead bodies. No eye hath seen
such scarecrows. I'll not march through Coventry with
them, that's flat: nay, and the villains march wide betwixt
the legs as if they had gyves on, for indeed I had the most
of them out of prison. There's not a shirt and a half in
40   all my company, and the half shirt is two napkins tacked
together and thrown over the shoulders like a herald's coat
without sleeves; and the shirt to say the truth stolen from
my host at Saint Albans, or the red-nose innkeeper of
Daventry. But that's all one, they'll find linen enough on
45   every hedge.

[*Enter the* **Prince** *and the* **Lord of Westmoreland**]

Prince   How now, blown Jack? How now, quilt?

Falstaff   What, Hal! How now, mad wag? What a devil
dost thou in Warwickshire? My good Lord of
Westmoreland, I cry you mercy, I thought your honour
50   had already been at Shrewsbury.

Westmoreland   Faith, Sir John, 'tis more than time that I
were there, and you too, but my powers are there already;
the King I can tell you looks for us all, we must away all
night.

Dives's dog. Such as never were soldiers – only servants sacked for dishonesty, men without inheritances, runaway barmen, grooms who've gone broke, and the unemployable. All ten times more dishonourably ragged than a tattered regimental flag is noble. Those I've replaced them with would make you think I'd got a hundred and fifty threadbare prodigal sons, all straight from pig-keeping: from eating pigswill and scraps. A clever-dick met me on the road here and told me I'd unloaded all the gallows and conscripted the corpses! Nobody's ever seen such scarecrows. I won't march through Coventry with them, that's for sure! The beggars march wide-legged, as if they had shackles on, 'cos I got most of them out of prisons. There's not a shirt and a half to be found in all my company, and the half shirt's a pair of handkerchiefs tied together and thrown over the shoulders like a herald's tabard. To tell you the truth, the shirt was stolen from the landlord at Saint Albans, or the red-nosed innkeeper in Daventry. It's all much of a muchness. They'll find all the clothes they need hanging out to dry on hedges.

[*Enter the* **Prince** *and* **Lord Westmoreland**]

Prince   How's things, Jack puff-and-pants? How goes it, fat-jacket?

Falstaff   Why, Hal! Greetings, mad-lad! What the devil are you doing in Warwickshire? [*He notices* **Lord Westmoreland**] Lord Westmoreland! I beg your pardon. I thought your honour was already at Shrewsbury . . .

Westmoreland   Indeed, Sir John, it's about time I was there, and you too – but my troops have arrived already. I can assure you the King is waiting for us all. We must travel through the night.

55 **Falstaff** Tut, never fear me, I am as vigilant as a cat to
steal cream.

Prince I think, to steal cream indeed, for thy theft hath
already made thee butter; but tell me, Jack, whose fellows
are these that come after?

60 **Falstaff** Mine, Hall, mine.

Prince I did never see such pitiful rascals.

Falstaff Tut, tut, good enough to toss, food for powder,
food for powder, they'll fill a pit as well as better; tush,
man, mortal men, mortal men.

65 **Westmoreland** Ay, but, Sir John, methinks they are
exceeding poor and bare, too beggarly.

Falstaff Faith, for their poverty I know not where they
had that; and for their bareness I am sure they never
learned that of me.

70 **Prince** No, I'll be sworn, unless you call three fingers in
the ribs bare. But sirrah, make haste; Percy is already in
the field.

[*Exit*]

Falstaff What, is the King encamped?

Westmoreland He is, Sir John, I fear we shall stay too
75   long.

[*Exit*]

Falstaff Well,
To the latter end of a fray, and the beginning of a feast

Falstaff   Trust me. I'll concentrate on it like a cat stealing cream.

Prince   Stealing cream is very apt: your theft has already turned you to butter! But tell me, Jack – whose men are these behind us? [*He points towards Falstaff's conscripts*]

Falstaff   Mine, Hal, mine.

Prince   I've never seen such pitiful wretches!

Falstaff   Tut – good enough for pike practice! Cannon-fodder, cannon-fodder! They'll fill a hole in the ground as well as their betters! Tush, man – they're living men, living men . . .

Westmoreland   Yes, Sir John, but I think they're incredibly poor and skinny; far too down-and-out . . .

Falstaff   'Strewth, I don't know where they got their poverty from, but I'm certain they didn't get their skinniness from me!

Prince   I'll vouch for that, unless you call three inches of fat 'skinny' . . . But get a move on, man; Percy has already taken up his position.

[*He goes*]

Falstaff   What – is the King camped too?

Westmoreland   He is, Sir John. I'm afraid we're losing time . . .

[*He goes*]

Falstaff   Well: 'The end of a fight and the start of a
                                                party

Fits a dull fighter and a keen guest.

[*Exit*]

Scene 3

Shrewsbury. The Rebel Camp. Enter **Hotspur, Worcester, Douglas, Vernon**

Hotspur   We'll fight with him tonight.

Worcester
It may not be.

Douglas   You give him then advantage.

Vernon
Not a whit.

Hotspur   Why say you so, looks he not for supply?

Vernon   So do we.

Hotspur   His is certain, ours is doubtful.

5 **Worcester**   Good cousin, be advised, stir not tonight.

Vernon   Do not, my lord.

Douglas
You do not counsel well.
You speak it out of fear and cold heart.

Vernon   Do me no slander, Douglas; by my life,
And I dare well maintain it with my life,
10   If well-respected honour bid me on,
I hold as little counsel with weak fear

Suit the soldier who's weak and the guest
who eats hearty'

[*He goes*]

Scene 3

The rebel camp at Shrewsbury. Enter **Hotspur, Worcester,
Douglas, Vernon**

Hotspur   We'll fight him tonight!

Worcester   Impossible!

Douglas   You'll give him an advantage then.

Vernon   Not at all.

Hotspur   Why do you say that? Isn't he expecting
reinforcements?

Vernon   So are we.

Hotspur   His are certain, ours doubtful.

Worcester   Cousin – be advised. Don't make a move
tonight.

Vernon   Don't my lord!

Douglas   Your advice isn't sound. It's based on fear and
half-heartedness.

Vernon   Don't slander me, Douglas! By my life – and I'll
put my life on the line to back this up – if wise counsel
recommends proceeding, I'll be as little influenced by

As you, my lord, or any Scot that this day lives;
Let it be seen tomorrow in the battle
Which of us fears.

Douglas   Yea, or tonight.

Vernon   Content.

15 **Hotspur**   Tonight, say I.

Vernon   Come, come, it may not be. I wonder much,
Being men of such great leading as you are,
That you foresee not what impediments
Drag back our expedition: certain horse
20 Of my cousin Vernon's are not yet come up,
Your uncle Worcester's horse came but today,
And now their pride and mettle is asleep,
Their courage with hard labour tame and dull,
That not a horse is half the half himself.

25 **Hotspur**   So are the horses of the enemy
In general journey-bated and brought low.
The better part of ours are full of rest.

Worcester   The number of the King exceedeth ours:
For God's sake, cousin, stay till all come in.

[*The trumpet sounds a parley*]

[*Enter* **Sir Walter Blunt**]

30 **Blunt**   I come with gracious offers from the King,
If you vouchsafe me hearing and respect.

Hotspur   Welcome, Sir Walter Blunt: and would to God
You were of our determination!
Some of us love you well, and even those some
35 Envy your great deservings and good name,
Because you are not of our quality,
But stand against us like an enemy.

fear as you, my lord, or any Scot alive today. Let's see tomorrow in the battle which of us shows fear.

Douglas   Yes, or tonight!

Vernon   Indeed.

Hotspur   I say – tonight.

Vernon   Come, come. That's not on. I'm surprised, you being men of such great generalship, that you can't see the snags that should hold us back. Some of my cousin's cavalry have not yet reached the front. Your Uncle Worcester's horses arrived only today. They're not in prime condition; their spirits are fatigued with over-exertion. No horse is a fraction of its best.

Hotspur   The enemy's horses are the same: travel-weary and exhausted. Most of ours have rested.

Worcester   The King outnumbers us. For God's sake, cousin, wait till everyone's here.

[*A trumpet sounds a parley.* **Sir Walter Blunt** *enters*]

Blunt   I come with gracious offers from the King, if you'll grant me a respectful hearing.

Hotspur   Welcome, Sir Walter Blunt. I wish to God you were one of us. Some of us regard you highly, even begrudging you your worthiness and reputation, because you are not of our party, but oppose us like an enemy.

Blunt   And God defend but still I should stand so,
So long as out of limit and true rule
You stand against anointed majesty.
40   But to my charge. The King hath sent to know
The nature of your griefs, and whereupon
You conjure from the breast of civil peace
Such bold hostility, teaching his duteous land
45   Audacious cruelty. If that the King
Have any way your good deserts forgot,
Which he confesseth to be manifold,
He bids you name your griefs, and with all speed
You shall have your desires with interest
50   And pardon absolute for yourself, and these
Herein misled by your suggestion.

Hotspur   The King is kind, and well we know the King
Knows at what time to promise, when to pay:
My father, and my uncle, and myself
55   Did give him that same royalty he wears,
And when he was not six and twenty strong,
Sick in the world's regard, wretched and low,
A poor unminded outlaw sneaking home,
My father gave him welcome to the shore:
60   And when he heard him swear and vow to God
He came but to be Duke of Lancaster,
To sue his livery, and beg his peace
With tears of innocency, and terms of zeal,
My father, in kind heart and pity moved,
65   Swore him assistance, and performed it too.
Now when the lords and barons of the realm
Perceived Northumberland did lean to him,
The more and less came in with cap and knee,
Met him in boroughs, cities, villages,
70   Attended him on bridges, stood in lanes,
Laid gifts before him, proffered him their oaths,
Gave him their heirs as pages, followed him

Blunt   And God forbid I'd be otherwise, so long as you stand against the anointed King, in breach of your allegiance and the law. But to my mission. The King wishes to know the nature of your grievances, and on what grounds you disturb the peace with such defiance, thereby corrupting his law-abiding subjects. If the King has in any way overlooked your merits, which he concedes are numerous, he bids you name your grievances, and with all speed you shall have what you are seeking, plus interest, and an absolute pardon for yourself and these others misled by your temptations.

Hotspur   How very kind of the King. We are well aware that the King knows when to promise, and when to pay . . . . My father, and my uncle, and myself gave him his crown: and when he was only a couple of dozen strong, unpopular, down on his luck, a poor unknown outlaw sneaking home, my father welcomed him to these shores. And when he heard him swear and vow to God that he only sought to be Duke of Lancaster, to recover his lands, and make his peace with the King by means of tears of innocence and words of loyalty, my father out of pity and a kind heart swore to assist him, and he did so, too. Now when the lords and barons of the realm saw that Northumberland favoured him, men of all ranks – cap in hand, on bended knee – met him in towns, cities, villages; waited for him on bridges, stood in lanes, laid gifts before him, offered him their allegiance, gave him their sons as pages, and followed at

Even at the heels in golden multitudes.
He presently, as greatness knows itself,
75   Steps me a little higher than his vow
Made to my father while his blood was poor
Upon the naked shore at Ravenspurgh;
And now forsooth takes on him to reform
Some certain edicts and some strait decrees
80   That lie too heavy on the commonwealth;
Cries out upon abuses, seems to weep
Over his country's wrongs; and by this face,
This seeming brow of justice, did he win
The hearts of all that he did angle for;
85   Proceeded further – cut me off the heads
Of all the favourites that the absent King
In deputation left behind him here,
When he was personal in the Irish war.

Blunt Tut, I came not to hear this.

Hotspur
                  Then to the point.
90   In short time after he deposed the King,
Soon after that deprived him of his life,
And in the neck of that tasked the whole state;
To make that worse, suffered his kinsman March
(Who is, if every owner were well placed,
95   Indeed his King) to be engaged in Wales,
There without ransom to lie forfeited;
Disgraced me in my happy victories,
Sought to entrap me by intelligence,
Rated mine uncle from the Council-board,
100   In rage dismissed my father from the court,
Broke oath on oath, committed wrong on wrong,
And in conclusion drove us to seek out
This head of safety, and withal to pry
Into his title, the which we find
105   Too indirect for long continuance.

his heels in adoring multitudes. Then in no time, as he recognized his own greatness, he goes a few steps further than the vow he made to my father, when his claim was weak, there on the bare shore at Ravenspurgh. Now, no less, he takes it on himself to reform some particular edicts, some strict decrees, that are a burden on the people. He denounces abuses: seems to weep over his country's wrongs. By putting on this face, this façade of apparent justice, he won the hearts of all whose help he wanted. And went one further . . . he chopped off the heads of all the favourites left behind as deputies by the absent Richard, while he was personally involved in the Irish war!

Blunt   Tut. I didn't come to listen to this.

Hotspur   To the point, then. Shortly after, he deposed the King. Soon after that, he took his life. And immediately following that, taxed the entire state. To make matters worse, he allowed his kinsman the Earl of March – who is, if everyone had their own, the true King – to be held as a hostage in Wales, where he lies forfeited for want of a ransom. He brought disgrace upon me in my fortunate victories: tried to trap me with spies; bawled my uncle out from the Privy Council; in a rage, banned my father from the Court; broke oath upon oath; committed wrong upon wrong. And finally, he drove us to devise this alliance in self-defence, and what's more to investigate his right to the throne, which we find too devious to last long.

Blunt   Shall I return this answer to the King?

Hotspur   Not so, Sir Walter. We'll withdraw awhile.
Go to the King, and let there be impawned
Some surety for a safe return again,
110   And in the morning early shall mine uncle
Bring him our purposes – and so, farewell.

Blunt   I would you would accept of grace and love.

Hotspur   And may be so we shall.

Blunt   Pray God you do.

[*Exeunt*]

Scene 4

York. The Archbishop's Palace. Enter the **Archbishop of
York** *and* **Sir Michael**

Archbishop   Hie, good Sir Michael, bear this sealed brief
With winged haste to the lord marshal,
This to my cousin Scroop, and all the rest
To whom they are directed. If you knew
5   How much they do import you would make haste.

Sir Michael   My good lord,
I guess their tenor.

Archbishop   Like enough you do.
Tomorrow, good Sir Michael, is a day
Wherein the fortune of ten thousand men
10   Must bide the touch; for, sir, at Shrewsbury,

Blunt   Is this the answer I'm to give to the King?

Hotspur   No, Sir Walter. We'll adjourn for a while. Go to the King. Early tomorrow morning my uncle will bring him our decision. Arrange a surety to guarantee his safe return. So, farewell.

Blunt   I wish you'd accept the grace and love that's offered you.

Hotspur   Perhaps we shall.

Blunt   Pray God you do.

[*They leave*]

Scene 4

The Archbishop's palace at York. Enter the **Archbishop of York** *and* **Sir Michael**

Archbishop   Go, good Sir Michael, and deliver this sealed letter with all speed to the Lord Marshall. Give this one to my cousin Scroop, all the others as addressed. If you knew how important they are, you'd hurry.

Sir Michael   My lord, I guess their subject matter.

Archbishop   No doubt you do. Tomorrow, good Sir Michael, is a day on which the fortunes of ten thousand men will be put to the test. As I understand it, the King

As I am truly given to understand,
The King with mighty and quick-raised power
Meets with Lord Harry: and I fear, Sir Michael,
What with the sickness of Northumberland,
15 Whose power was in the first proportion,
And what with Owen Glendower's absence thence,
Who with them was a rated sinew too,
And comes not in, o'er-ruled by prophecies,
I fear the power of Percy is too weak
20 To wage an instant trial with the King.

Sir Michael   Why, my good lord, you need not fear,
There is Douglas, and Lord Mortimer.

Archbishop   No, Mortimer is not there.

Sir Michael   But there is Mordake, Vernon, Lord Harry
Percy,
25 And there is my Lord of Worcester, and a head
Of gallant warriors, noble gentlemen.

Archbishop   And so there is: but yet the King hath drawn
The special head of all the land together:
The Prince of Wales, Lord John of Lancaster,
30 The noble Westmoreland, and warlike Blunt,
And many moe corrivals and dear men
Of estimation and command in arms.

Sir Michael   Doubt not, my lord, they shall be well
opposed.

35 **Archbishop**   I hope no less, yet needful 'tis to fear;
And to prevent the worst, Sir Michael, speed.
For if Lord Percy thrive not, ere the King
Dismiss his power he means to visit us,
For he hath heard of our confederacy,
And 'tis but wisdom to make strong against him:
40 Therefore make haste – I must go write again
To other friends; and so, farewell, Sir Michael.

[*Exeunt*]

and the mighty army he so quickly raised joins with Lord Harry at Shrewsbury, and I fear, Sir Michael, that what with the sickness of Northumberland, whose army was the major one – and what with the absence of Owen Glendower – another important contributor, but missing because some prophecies have over-ruled him – I fear the forces of Percy are too weak to challenge the King right now.

Sir Michael   Why, my good lord, you need have no worry. There is Douglas. And Lord Mortimer.

Archbishop   No. Mortimer is not there.

Sir Michael   But there's Mordake, Vernon, Lord Harry Percy – and there's my Lord of Worcester – and an army of gallant warriors and noble gentlemen.

Archbishop   And so there is: but the King, however, has gathered a country-wide army together: the Prince of Wales, Lord John of Lancaster, the noble Westmoreland, the warlike Blunt, and many more associates, and honourable men of worth, and brothers in arms.

Sir Michael   Have no doubt, my lord, that they'll be well opposed.

Archbishop   That's my hope, but one cannot but fear. And to prevent the worst, Sir Michael, make haste! Because if Lord Percy doesn't prosper, before the King disbands his army he intends to visit us. He's heard of our being part of the alliance, and it's only wise to arm up against him. So hurry. I must go and write to other friends. Farewell, then, Sir Michael.

[*They go*]

Act five

Scene 1

Shrewsbury. The King's Camp. Enter the **King**, **Prince of Wales, Lord John of Lancaster, Sir Walter Blunt, Falstaff.**

King How bloodily the sun begins to peer
Above yon bulky hill! The day looks pale
At his distemp'rature.

Prince   The southern wind
Doth play the trumpet to his purposes,
5   And by his hollow whistling in the leaves
Foretells a tempest and a blust'ring day.

King Then with the losers let it sympathise,
For nothing can seem foul to those that win.

[The trumpet sounds]

[Enter **Worcester** *and* **Vernon**]

How now, my Lord of Worcester! 'Tis not well
10   That you and I should meet upon such terms
As now we meet. You have deceived our trust,
And made us doff our easy robes of peace
To crush our old limbs in ungentle steel:
This is not well, my lord, this is not well.
15   What say you to it? Will you again unknit
This churlish knot of all-abhorred war,
And move in that obedient orb again
Where you did give a fair and natural light,
And be no more an exhaled meteor,
20   A prodigy of fear, and a portent
Of broached mischief to the unborn times?

Act five

Scene 1

The King's camp at Shrewsbury. Enter the **King**, *the* **Prince of Wales**, **Lord John of Lancaster**, **Sir Walter Blunt** *and* **Falstaff**

King   How blood-red the sun is as it begins to peep over that bulky hill! Its feverish look makes day seem pale.

Prince   A southern wind announces its approach. The hollow whistling through the leaves foretells a stormy and a blustery day.

King   The losers will find it apt. To those who win, nothing is disagreeable.

[*A trumpet sounds.* **Worcester** *and* **Vernon** *enter*]

Well now, my Lord of Worcester. It's a matter of regret that you and I should meet upon the present terms. You have betrayed our trust. Now we must take off our comfortable, peacetime robes and crush our old limbs into rigid armour. I don't like it, my lord. I don't like it. What's your message? Will you disengage from hateful war, and return again to your respected place as part of the loyal establishment – ceasing to be a dissident, a potential threat, and a portent of further mischief in days to come?

Worcester Hear me, my liege:
For mine own part I could be well content
To entertain the lag end of my life
25 With quiet hours. For I protest
I have not sought the day of this dislike.

King You have not sought it? How comes it, then?

Falstaff Rebellion lay in his way, and he found it.

Prince Peace, chewet, peace!

30 **Worcester** It pleased your Majesty to turn your looks
Of favour from myself, and all our house,
And yet I must remember you, my lord,
We were the first and dearest of your friends;
For you my staff of office did I break
35 In Richard's time, and posted day and night
To meet you on the way, and kiss your hand,
When yet you were in place and in account
Nothing so strong and fortunate as I.
It was myself, my brother, and his son,
40 That brought you home, and boldly did outdare
The dangers of the time. You swore to us,
And you did swear that oath at Doncaster,
That you did nothing purpose 'gainst the state,
Nor claim no further than your new-fall'n right,
45 The seat of Gaunt, dukedom of Lancaster.
To this we swore our aid: but in short space
It rained down fortune show'ring on your head,
And such a flood of greatness fell on you,
What with our help, what with the absent King,
50 What with the injuries of a wanton time,
The seeming sufferances that you had borne,
And the contrarious winds that held the King
So long in his unlucky Irish wars
That all in England did repute him dead:
55 And from this swarm of fair advantages

Worcester   With respect, my liege: for myself, I'd be happy
to take things easy in my latter days. I must say I haven't
sought this present disfavour.

King   You haven't sought it? How did it come about, then?

Falstaff   Rebellion got in his way and he bumped into it!

Prince   Quiet, chatterbox! Quiet!

Worcester   It pleased your majesty to cease to look with
favour on myself and my family. But I must remind you,
my lord, that we were the first and the closest of your
friends. For you, I resigned from high office in King
Richard's time, and raced by day and night to meet you
on your arrival, and kiss your hand. Then you were
neither so strong nor so fortunate as I in status and in
reputation. It was myself, my brother and his son who
brought you home, and boldly disregarded the dangers of
that time. You gave us your oath, and swore it at
Doncaster, that you had no designs against the state; no
claim beyond John of Gaunt's estate, the newly-vacant
Dukedom of Lancaster. To this we pledged our aid. But
very soon you were deluged with good luck. A veritable
flood of greatness descended on you – what with our
help, and what with the King's absence, and what with
the grievances of misgovernment, and the apparent
injustices you had suffered, and the contrary winds that
kept the King so long in his unlucky Irish wars that
everyone in England thought he was dead. . . . And with
these blessings swarming in on you, you grabbed the

213

You took occasion to be quickly wooed
To gripe the general sway into your hand,
Forgot your oath to us at Doncaster,
And being fed by us, you used us so
60   As that ungentle gull the cuckoo's bird
Useth the sparrow – did oppress our nest,
Grew by our feeding to so great a bulk
That even our love durst not come near your sight
For fear of swallowing; but with nimble wing
65   We were enforced for safety sake to fly
Out of your sight, and raise this present head,
Whereby we stand opposed by such means
As you yourself have forged against yourself,
By unkind usage, dangerous countenance,
70   And violation of all faith and troth
Sworn to us in your younger enterprise.

King   These things indeed you have articulate,
Proclaimed at market crosses, read in churches,
To face the garment of rebellion
75   With some fine colour that may please the eye
Of fickle changelings and poor discontents,
Which gape and rub the elbow at the news
Of hurlyburly innovation;
And never yet did insurrection want
80   Such water-colours to impaint his cause,
Nor moody beggars starving for a time
Of pellmell havoc and confusion.

Prince   In both your armies there is many a soul
Shall pay full dearly for this encounter
85   If once they join in trial. Tell your nephew,
The Prince of Wales doth join with all the world
In praise of Henry Percy: by my hopes,
This present enterprise set off his head,
I do not think a braver gentleman,

initiative, forgot your oath to us at Doncaster, and having been nourished by us, you used us like the ungrateful young cuckoo does the sparrow. You took us over, and grew so big from feeding off us that even we who loved you didn't dare approach for fear of being gobbled up. For safety's sake, we were forced to fly off swiftly out of your sight, and raise this present army. Our opposition is of your own making – the consequence of your ingratitude, your threatening manner, and the betrayal of all the faith and trust you swore to us in your early days.

King   These things you have indeed spelled out, and proclaimed at market places, and read in churches, to make your rebellion superficially appealing to the fickle turncoats and wretched malcontents who wallow in rumours of anarchy. Rebellion is never lacking in such wishy-washy tints to colour its cause, or short of sullen have-nots yearning for a spell of unbridled anarchy and chaos!

Prince   In both our armies there is many a man who'll pay with his life for this confrontation, if it comes to war. Tell your nephew that the Prince of Wales joins with the rest of the world in praising Henry Percy. This present matter excepted, upon my precious soul I do not think that a braver gentleman, more actively valiant or more valiant

90   More active-valiant or more valiant-young,
        More daring or more bold, is now alive
        To grace this latter age with noble deeds.
        For my part, I may speak it to my shame,
        I have a truant been to chivalry,
95   And so I hear he doth account me too;
        Yet this before my father's majesty –
        I am content that he shall take the odds
        Of his great name and estimation,
        And will, to save the blood on either side,
100   Try fortune with him in a single fight.

   King   And, Prince of Wales, so dare we venture thee
        Albeit, considerations infinite
        Do make against it: no, good Worcester, no,
        We love our people well, even those we love
105   That are misled upon your cousin's part,
        And will they take the offer of our grace,
        Both he, and they, and you, yea, every man
        Shall be my friend again, and I'll be his:
        So tell your cousin, and bring me word
110   What he will do. But if he will not yield,
        Rebuke and dread correction wait on us,
        And they shall do their office. So, be gone;
        We will not now be troubled with reply:
        We offer fair, take it advisedly.

                        [*Exit* **Worcester** *with* **Vernon**]

115 **Prince**   It will not be accepted, on my life;
        The Douglas and the Hotspur both together
        Are confident against the world in arms.

   King   Hence, therefore, every leader to his charge;
        For on their answer will we set on them,
120   And God befriend us as our cause is just!

[*Exeunt all but the* **Prince** *and* **Falstaff**]

for his age – more daring, or more bold – is living today
to bring glory to our generation. For myself, and I speak
this to my shame, I've been a stranger to chivalry, and I
hear that's his opinion of me, too. But I say this in the
presence of my father the King: I'll concede him favourite
on account of his great name and reputation, and, to
save lives on either side, I'll challenge him to single
combat.

King   And, Prince of Wales, we'll back you, though there's
every reason why we shouldn't. No, good Worcester, no.
We love our people greatly, even those your nephew has
misled. If they will take the offer of our clemency, then
he, and they, and you – yes, everyone – shall be my
friend again and I'll be his. Tell this to your nephew,
and bring me word what he intends to do. If he will not
comply, then disapproval and stern punishment are at
our service, and they'll do their duty. So, be gone. We do
not wish to be troubled now with your reply. Our offer is
fair: we advise you to take it.

[*Exit* **Worcester** *and* **Vernon**]

Prince   I'll bet my life they will not take it. Douglas and
Hotspur in alliance will confidently take on the world.

King   Go, therefore, every leader to his command. When
they reply, we'll attack – and God be our friend, as our
cause is just!

[*They all leave but the* **Prince** *and* **Falstaff**]

Falstaff   Hal, if thou see me down in the battle and
    bestride me, so; 'tis a point of friendship.

Prince   Nothing but a Colossus can do thee that friendship.
    Say thy prayers, and farewell.

125 **Falstaff**   I would 'twere bed-time, Hal, and all well.

Prince   Why, thou owest God a death.

[*Exit*]

Falstaff   'Tis not due yet, I would be loath to pay him
    before his day – what need I be so forward with him that
    calls not on me? Well, 'tis no matter, honour pricks me
130   on. Yea, but how if honour prick me off when I come on,
    how then? Can honour set to a leg? No. Or an arm? No.
    Or take away the grief of a wound? No. Honour hath no
    skill in surgery then? No. What is honour? A word. What
    is in that word honour? What is that honour? Air. A trim
135   reckoning! Who hath it? He that died a-Wednesday. Doth
    he feel it? No. Doth he hear it? No. 'Tis insensible, then?
    Yea, to the dead. But will it not live with the living? No.
    Why? Detraction will not suffer it. Therefore I'll none
    of it. Honour is a mere scutcheon – and so ends my
140   catechism.

[*Exit*]

Falstaff   Hal, if you see me fall in battle, stand over me. That's what friendship is all about.

Prince   Nothing short of a Colossus could do you that friendship! Say your prayers, and farewell!

Falstaff   I wish it were bed-time, Hal, and all was well.

Prince   Why – you owe God a death!

[*He goes*]

Falstaff   It's not due yet. I'd be loath to pay him before the day of reckoning. Why should I pay in advance when I haven't had the bill? Well, it doesn't matter. Honour spurs me on. [*He thinks*] Yes – but what if honour spurs me off once I'm on? How about that? Can honour set a broken leg? No. Or an arm? Or take away the pain of a wound? No. Honour has no skill in surgery, then? No. What is honour? A word. What's in that word 'honour'? What is that honour? Air! A fine reward! Who has it? The man who died last Wednesday . . . Does he feel it? No. Does he hear it? No. It's insubstantial, then? Yes – to the dead. But won't it live with the living? No. Why? Slander destroys it. Therefore I'll have nothing to do with it. Honour is merely an epitaph. And that ends my cross-questioning!

Scene 2

Shrewsbury. The Rebel Camp. Enter **Worcester** *and* **Sir Richard Vernon**

Worcester   O no, my nephew must not know, Sir Richard,
The liberal and kind offer of the King.

Vernon   'Twere best he did.

Worcester   Then are we all undone.
It is not possible, it cannot be,
5   The King should keep his word in loving us;
He will suspect us still, and find a time
To punish this offence in other faults:
Supposition all our lives shall be stuck full of eyes,
For treason is but trusted like the fox,
10   Who, never so tame, so cherished and locked up,
Will have a wild trick of his ancestors.
Look how we can, or sad or merrily,
Interpretation will misquote our looks,
And we shall feed like oxen at a stall,
15   The better cherished still the nearer death.
My nephew's trespass may be well forgot,
It hath the excuse of youth and heat of blood,
And an adopted name of privilege –
A hare-brained Hotspur, governed by a spleen:
20   All his offences live upon my head
And on his father's. We did train him on,
And, his corruption being ta'en from us,
We as the spring of all shall pay for all:
Therefore, good cousin, let not Harry know
25   In any case the offer of the King.

Vernon   Deliver what you will; I'll say 'tis so.
Here comes your cousin.

Scene 2

The rebel camp at Shrewsbury. Enter **Worcester** *and* **Sir Richard Vernon**

Worcester   Oh, no. My nephew must not know, Sir Richard, of the King's liberal and kind offer.

Vernon   He ought to be told.

Worcester   Then we'd all be done for. It's impossible, it simply could not be, that the King would keep his word in loving us. He'll always suspect us, and find a time when he can punish this offence through other faults. All our lives we'll be eyed with suspicion. Treason is trusted like we trust a fox. No matter how tame it is, or well-cared for, or kept locked up, it will retain the cunning of its ancestors. No matter how we look, sad or cheerful, our looks will be misinterpreted. We'll be like oxen feeding at a stall: the more we're well-treated, the closer we'll be to death. My nephew's misdemeanour may well be forgotten; it has the excuse of youth, and hot blood; and his nickname gives him privileges – he's the harebrained Hotspur, given to rash outbursts. All his offences will be attributed to me, and to his father. We trained him, and as he caught his corruption from us, as the source of it all we'll pay the penalty for it all. Therefore, good cousin, don't whatever you do let Harry know of the King's offer.

Vernon   Tell him what you want. I'll back you up. Here comes your nephew.

[*Enter* **Hotspur** *and* **Douglas**]

Hotspur   My uncle is returned;
    Deliver up my Lord of Westmoreland.
    Uncle, what news?

30 **Worcester**   The King will bid you battle presently.

Douglas   Defy him by the Lord of Westmoreland.

Hotspur   Lord Douglas, go you and tell him so.

Douglas   Marry, and shall, and very willingly.

[*Exit*]

Worcester   There is no seeming mercy in the King.

35 **Hotspur**   Did you beg any? God forbid!

Worcester   I told him gently of our grievances,
    Of his oath-breaking; which he mended thus,
    By now forswearing that he is forsworn:
    He calls us rebels, traitors, and will scourge
40   With haughty arms this hateful name in us.

[*Re-enter* **Douglas**]

Douglas   Arm, gentlemen, to arms! for I have thrown
    A brave defiance in King Henry's teeth,
    And Westmoreland that was engaged did bear it,
    Which cannot choose but bring him quickly on.

45 **Worcester**   The Prince of Wales stepped forth before the
    King,
    And, nephew, challenged you to single fight.

Hotspur   O, would the quarrel lay upon our heads,
    And that no man might draw short breath today

[*Enter* **Hotspur** *and* **Douglas**]

Hotspur   My uncle has returned. Release his hostage, the Lord of Westmoreland. Well, uncle: what news?

Worcester   The King will call you to battle immediately.

Douglas   Send your defiance through Lord Westmoreland!

Hotspur   Lord Douglas, go and tell him so.

Douglas   Indeed I shall, and very willingly!

[*He goes*]

Worcester   There's no sign of mercy in the King.

Hotspur   Did you beg any? God forbid!

Worcester   I told him calmly of our grievances, and of his broken promises. He responded by denying that he'd promised anything. He called us rebels and traitors, and says he'll thrash those hateful qualities in us with his royal forces.

[**Douglas** *returns*]

Douglas   Arm, gentlemen! To arms! I've sent King Henry a contemptuous challenge and Westmoreland who stood as hostage has conveyed it. It's bound to provoke a quick response.

Worcester   The Prince of Wales stood before the King and, nephew, he challenged you to single combat.

Hotspur   Would that the quarrel were between us only, and that nobody but Harry Monmouth and I should gasp for

But I and Harry Monmouth! Tell me, tell me,
50   How showed his tasking? Seemed it in contempt?

Vernon   No, by my soul, I never in my life
Did hear a challenge urged more modestly,
Unless a brother should a brother dare
To gentle exercise and proof of arms.
55   He gave you all the duties of a man,
Trimmed up your praises with a princely tongue,
Spoke your deservings like a chronicle,
Making you ever better than his praise
By still dispraising praise valued with you,
60   And, which became him like a prince indeed,
He made a blushing cital of himself,
And chid his truant youth with such a grace
As if he mastered there a double spirit
Of teaching and of learning instantly.
65   There did he pause: but let me tell the world –
If he outlive the envy of this day,
England did never owe so sweet a hope
So much misconstrued in his wantonness.

Hotspur   Cousin, I think thou art enamoured
70   On his follies: never did I hear
Of any prince so wild a liberty.
But be he as he will, yet once ere night
I will embrace him with a soldier's arm,
That he shall shrink under my courtesy.
75   Arm, arm with speed! And fellows, soldiers, friends,
Better consider what you have to do
Than I that have not well the gift of tongue
Can lift your blood up with persuasion.

[*Enter a* **Messenger**]

Messenger   My lord, here are letters for you.

224

breath today! Tell me, tell me: what was his challenge like? Did it seem contemptuous?

Vernon   No, upon my soul. I never in all my life heard a challenge expressed more politely, short of a brother daring a brother to a friendly contest. He gave you full respect as man to man. He sang your praises in a princely way. He spoke of your fine qualities like a history book, making you out to be even better than his praises by disparaging praise, because it couldn't do you justice. And what really became him like the prince he is, he blushingly accused himself, rebuking his mis-spent youth so sincerely that at one and the same time he mastered both the art of teaching and of learning. There he stopped. But let me tell the world: if he should outlive today's hostilities, England never had so promising a prospect so misunderstood by his wayward living.

Hotspur   Cousin, I think you've taken a fancy to his follies! I've never heard of a prince so wild a libertine. But be that as it may, before this day ends I'll give him such a soldierly embrace he'll be embarrassed by my ardour! To arms – and instantly! And – comrades, soldiers, friends! – I haven't got the gift of the gab to get your blood up; you know what has to be done . . .

[*A* **Messenger** *enters*]

Messenger   Here are letters for you, my lord.

80 **Hotspur**   I cannot read them now.
    O gentlemen, the time of life is short!
    To spend that shortness basely were too long
    If life did ride upon a dial's point,
    Still ending at the arrival of an hour.
85   And if we live, we live to tread on kings,
    If die, brave death when princes die with us!
    Now, for our consciences, the arms are fair
    When the intent of bearing them is just.

[*Enter another* **Messenger**]

Messenger   My lord, prepare, the King comes on apace.

90 **Hotspur**   I thank him that he cuts me from my tale,
    For I profess not talking: only this –
    Let each man do his best; and here draw I
    A sword whose temper I intend to stain
    With the best blood that I can meet withal
95   In the adventure of this perilous day.
    Now, Esperance! Percy! and set on,
    Sound all the lofty instruments of war,
    And by that music let us all embrace,
    For, heaven to earth, some of us never shall
100   A second time do such a courtesy.

[*Here they embrace, the trumpets sound, exeunt*]

Hotspur   I can't read them now. Gentlemen: life is short. If it lasted only an hour, it would be overlong if lived dishonourably. Should we live, we live to humble kings. Should we die, what finer death than in the company of princes! As for our consciences, war is righteous when the cause is just!

[*Another* **Messenger** *enters*]

Messenger   Make ready, my lord: the King is advancing quickly.

Hotspur   I'm grateful to him for cutting me short. I'm no talker. Just this – let every man do his best. I draw my sword, intending to stain its blade with the best blood I can encounter in today's perilous struggle. So [*he shouts his rallying cry*] 'Hope be my comfort! Percy!' and advance! Sound all the fanfares of war, and let us all embrace to that music! Some of us won't live to do so again, that's for certain!

[*They exchange embraces. The trumpets sound, and they leave for the battlefield*]

Scene 3

*Shrewsbury. The field of battle. The **King** enters with his power. Alarum to the battle. Then enter **Douglas**, and **Sir Walter Blunt** disguised as the King*

Blunt   What is thy name that in the battle thus
Thou crossest me? What honour dost thou seek
Upon my head?

Douglas   Knowest then my name is Douglas,
And I do haunt thee in the battle thus
5   Because some tell me that thou art a king.

Blunt   They tell thee true.

Douglas   The Lord of Stafford dear today hath bought
Thy likeness, for instead of thee, King Harry,
This sword hath ended him: so shall it thee
10   Unless thou yield thee as my prisoner.

Blunt   I was not born a yielder, thou proud Scot,
And thou shalt find a king that will revenge
Lord Stafford's death.

[*They fight. **Douglas** kills **Blunt***]

[*Then enter **Hotspur***]

Hotspur   O Douglas, hadst thou fought at Holmedon thus
15   I never had triumphed upon a Scot.

Douglas   All's done, all's won: here breathless lies the
King.

Hotspur   Where?

Douglas   Here.

Scene 3

The battlefield at Shrewsbury. The **King** *crosses the stage with his forces.* **Douglas** *enters, and* **Sir Walter Blunt** *disguised as the* **King**

Blunt   Your name, since you cross me in battle! What honour do you hope to gain through me?

Douglas   My name is Douglas. I've sought you out in the battle because I'm told you are the King.

Blunt   You've heard the truth.

Douglas   Today, Lord Stafford has paid dearly for impersonation. Instead of you, King Harry, this sword has ended him. Unless you surrender as my prisoner, you too shall die!

Blunt   I wasn't born a yielder, proud Scot! You'll discover I'm a King who'll revenge Lord Stafford's life.

[*They fight.* **Blunt** *is killed*]

[**Hotspur** *enters*]

Hotspur   Douglas, if you had fought like this at Holmedon, I never would have defeated the Scots.

Douglas   All's done. All's won! Here lies the King, dead!

Hotspur   Where?

Douglas   Here.

Hotspur   This, Douglas? No, I know this face full well,
A gallant knight he was, his name was Blunt,
20   Semblably furnished like the King himself.

Douglas   A fool go with thy soul, whither it goes!
A borrowed title hast thou bought too dear.
Why didst thou tell me that thou wert a king?

25 **Hotspur**   The King hath many marching in his coats.

Douglas   Now, by my sword, I will kill all his coats;
I'll murder all his wardrobe, piece by piece,
Until I meet the King.

Hotspur   Up and away!
Our soldiers stand full fairly for the day.

                                                          [*Exeunt*]

[*Alarum. Enter* **Falstaff** *solus*]

30 **Falstaff**   Though I could scape shot-free at London, I fear
the shot here, here's no scoring but upon the pate. Soft!
who are you? Sir Walter Blunt – there's honour for you!
Here's no vanity! I am as hot as molten lead, and as heavy
too: God keep lead out of me, I need no more weight than
35   mine own bowels. I have led my ragamuffins where they
are peppered; there's not three of my hundred and fifty left
alive, and they are for the town's end, to beg during life.
But who comes here?

[*Enter the* **Prince**]

40 **Prince**   What, stands thou idle here? Lend me thy sword:
Many a nobleman lies stark and stiff
Under the hoofs of vaunting enemies,
Whose deaths are yet unrevenged. I prithee lend me thy
     sword.

Hotspur   This, Douglas? No. I know this face very well. He
was a gallant knight. His name was Blunt. He and the
King were dressed alike.

Douglas   [*To* **Blunt's** *corpse*] Wherever your soul may be,
it's with a fool! You paid too high a price for that
borrowed title. Why did you tell me you were the King?

Hotspur   The King has many decoys wearing his heraldic
coats.

Douglas   Upon my sword, I'll kill all his coats! I'll murder
his entire wardrobe, piece by piece, until I find the King!

Hotspur   Let's be going. Our soldiers seem to be winning.

   [*They go*]

   [**Falstaff** *enters amid the noise of battle*]

Falstaff   In London, I could dodge paying my account.
Here, I'm afraid of going to my account. You can't get
into the red here – unless you're given a bleeding head!
[*He sees* **Blunt's** *body*] Hello! Who are you? Sir Walter
Blunt! Now there's honour for you! Folly indeed! I feel as
hot as molten lead, and as heavy, too. But God keep me
free from lead! My own stomach is weighty enough. I've
led my ragamuffins where they've been massacred – not
three of my hundred and fifty are still alive. And they're
for the gutter, to beg for the rest of their lives. But who
comes here?

   [*The* **Prince** *enters*]

Prince   What, are you standing here idle? Lend me your
sword. Many a nobleman lies stiff and stark beneath the
hoofs of boastful enemies, their deaths not yet revenged.
Please, lend me your sword!

Falstaff O Hal, I prithee give me leave to breathe
awhile – Turk Gregory never did such deeds in arms as I
45 have done this day; I have paid Percy, I have made him
sure.

Prince He is indeed, and living to kill thee: I prithee lend
me thy sword.

Falstaff Nay, before God, Hal, if Percy be alive thou gets
50 not my sword, but take my pistol if thou wilt.

Prince Give it me: what, is it in the case?

Falstaff Ay, Hal, 'tis hot, 'tis hot; there's that will sack a
city.

[*The* **Prince** *draws it out, and find it to be a bottle of sack*]

Prince What, is it a time to jest and dally now?

[*He throws the bottle at him. Exit*]

55 **Falstaff** Well, if Percy be alive, I'll pierce him. If he do
come in my way, so: if he do not, if I come in his
willingly, let him make a carbonado of me. I like not such
grinning honour as Sir Walter hath. Give me life, which if
I can save, so: if not, honour comes unlooked for, and
60 there's an end.

[*Exit*]

Falstaff   Oh, Hal, please let me get my breath back. Ruthless Pope Gregory never did such valorous deeds as I have done today. I've killed Percy. I've made sure of him.

Prince   He's very much alive, and able to kill you. I beg you, lend me your sword.

Falstaff   Well now, before God, Hal: if Percy's alive, you're not getting my sword. But take my pistol if you wish.

Prince   Give it me. [**Falstaff** *hands over a pistol case*] What – is it still in its case?

Falstaff   Yes, Hal, it's hot, it's hot. What's there would sack a city.

[*The* **Prince** *opens the case and finds a bottle of 'sack' – white wine – in it*]

Prince   Is this a time for idle jokes? [*He throws the bottle at him and returns to the battle*]

Falstaff   Well, if Percy's still alive, I'll pierce him! If he crosses my path, so be it. If he doesn't, and I cross his willingly, I'm his for mincemeat! I don't like the kind of grisly honour that Sir Walter has. Give me life. If I can save it, great. If not, honour will be thrust upon me, and that'll be the end of it.

[*He goes*]

Scene 4

The Same. Alarum. Excursions. Enter the **King**, *the* **Prince,**
Lord John of Lancaster, Earl of Westmoreland

King   I prithee, Harry, withdraw thyself, thou bleed'st too
    much.
    Lord John of Lancaster, go you with him.

Lancaster   Not I, my lord, unless I did bleed too.

Prince   I beseech your Majesty, make up,
5   Lest your retirement do amaze your friends.

King   I will do so. My Lord of Westmoreland,
    Lead him to his tent.

Westmoreland   Come, my lord, I'll lead you to your tent.

Prince   Lead me, my lord? I do not need your help,
10   And God forbid a shallow scratch should drive
    The Prince of Wales from such a field as this,
    Where stained nobility lies trodden on,
    And rebels' arms triumph in massacres!

Lancaster   We breathe too long: come, cousin
        Westmoreland,
15   Our duty this way lies: for God's sake, come.

[*Exeunt* **Lancaster** *and* **Westmoreland**]

Prince   By God, thou hast deceived me, Lancaster,
    I did not think thee lord of such a spirit:
    Before, I loved thee as a brother, John,
    But now I do respect thee as my soul.

20 **King**   I saw him hold Lord Percy at the point

Scene 4

The battlefield. The **King** *enters, followed by the* **Prince,** **Lord John of Lancaster** *and the* **Earl of Westmoreland**

King Harry, please: withdraw. You are bleeding too much! Lord John of Lancaster, go with him.

Lancaster Not unless I was bleeding too, my lord.

Prince I beg your Majesty: move up to the battlefront in case your absence dismays your friends.

King I'll do that. My Lord of Westmoreland, escort him to his tent.

Westmoreland Come, my lord. I'll escort you to your tent.

Prince Escort me, my lord? I don't need your help. God forbid that a superficial scratch should drive the Prince of Wales from a battlefield such as this: where fallen noblemen are trodden underfoot, and rebel forces massacre in triumph.

Lancaster We've rested too long. Come, cousin Westmoreland: our duty lies in this direction. For God's sake, come!

[**Lancaster** *and* **Westmoreland** *return to the battle*]

Prince By God, Lancaster, you've had me folded! I didn't think you boasted so much courage. Before, I've loved you as a brother, John. Now you are a soul-mate!

King I saw him tackle Lord Percy with more

235

With lustier maintenance than I did look for
Of such an ungrown warrior.

Prince   O, this boy
Lends mettle to us all!

                                                                [*Exit*]

[*Enter* **Douglas**]

Douglas   Another king! They grow like Hydra's heads:
25   I am the Douglas, fatal to all those
That wear those colours on them. What art thou
That counterfeit'st the person of a king?

King   The King himself, who, Douglas, grieves at heart
So many of his shadows thou hast met,
30   And not the very King. I have two boys
Seek Percy and thyself about the field,
But seeing thou fall'st on me so luckily
I will assay thee, and defend thyself.

Douglas   I fear thou art another counterfeit,
35   And yet, in faith, thou bearest thee like a king;
But mine I am sure thou art, whoe'er thou be,
And thus I win thee.

[*They fight, the* **King** *being in danger*]

[*Enter* **Prince of Wales**]

Prince   Hold up thy head, vile Scot, or thou art like
Never to hold it up again! The spirits
40   Of valiant Shirley, Stafford, Blunt are in my arms.
It is the Prince of Wales that threatens thee,
Who never promiseth but he means to pay.

[*They fight:* **Douglas** *runs away*]

Cheerly, my lord, how fares your grace?

determined guts than I could have expected from so young a warrior!

Prince   Oh, this boy inspires us!

[*He goes*]

[**Douglas** *enters. He recognizes the royal coat of arms*]

Douglas   Another King! The more they're slain, the more there are of them! I am Douglas: I bring death to all who wear those colours! Who are you, pretending to be King?

King   The King himself, who's heartsick that you've met so many doubles, and not the real King. I have two sons who are searching for you and Percy on the battlefield, but seeing luck has brought you to me, I'll take you on. Defend yourself!

Douglas   I suspect you're another counterfeit, though you do have a kingly bearing. Whoever you are, you're mine for sure, so I'll take you! [*He crosses swords with the* **King**, *who is quickly in trouble*]

[*The* **Prince of Wales** *returns*]

Prince   Hold it there, you Scottish villain, or you'll never live to hold another thing! I fight to avenge the deaths of Shirley, Stafford and Blunt. It's the Prince of Wales who challenges you, who never makes a promise he can't keep!

[*They fight.* **Douglas** *runs away*]

Courage, my lord! How are you, sir? Sir Nicholas

45 Sir Nicholas Gawsey hath for succour sent,
And so hath Clifton – I'll to Clifton straight.

King   Stay and breathe a while:
Thou hast redeemed thy lost opinion,
And showed thou mak'st some tender of my life,
In this fair rescue thou hast brought to me.

50 **Prince**   O God, they did me too much injury
That ever said I hearkened for your death.
If it were so, I might have let alone
The insulting hand of Douglas over you,
Which would have been as speedy in your end
55 As all the poisonous potions in the world,
And saved the treacherous labour of your son.

King   Make up to Clifton, I'll to Sir Nicholas Gawsey.

[*Exit*]

[*Enter* **Hotspur**]

Hotspur   If I mistake not, thou art Harry Monmouth.

Prince   Thou speakest as if I would deny my name.

60 **Hotspur**   My name is Harry Percy.

Prince
                              Why then I see
A very valiant rebel of the name.
I am the Prince of Wales, and think not, Percy,
To share with me in glory any more:
Two stars keep not their motion in one sphere,
65 Nor can one England brook a double reign
Of Harry Percy and the Prince of Wales.

Hotspur   Nor shall it, Harry, for the hour is come
To end the one of us, and would to God
Thy name in arms were now as great as mine!

Gawsey has sent for help, and so has Clifton. I'll go
to Clifton right now.

King   Stay and catch your breath. You have regained
your lost reputation, and proved you have concern
for my wellbeing in coming to my rescue.

Prince   My God, they went too far when they said I
wished you dead! Had that been so, I could have
ignored the triumphant Douglas when he
overpowered you. That would have killed you
quicker than all the poisonous potions in the world
– and saved your son the treacherous trouble!

King   You go to Clifton. I'll help Sir Nicholas Gawsey.

[*The* **King** *leaves*]

[**Hotspur** *enters*]

Hotspur   Harry Monmouth, if I'm not mistaken!

Prince   You say it as though I'd deny my name.

Hotspur   Mine is Harry Percy.

Prince   Why, then I'm looking at a very valiant rebel
of that name. I am the Prince of Wales. Give up the
thought of sharing my renown. No two stars can
occupy the same orbit: nor can England tolerate the
dual reign of Harry Percy and the Prince of Wales.

Hotspur   Nor will it, Harry – the time has come for
one of us to die. Would to God that as a warrior
your name was ranked like mine!

70 **Prince**   I'll make it greater ere I part from thee,
      And all the budding honours on thy crest
      I'll crop to make a garland for my head.

Hotspur   I can no longer brook thy vanities.

   [*They fight*]

   [*Enter* **Falstaff**]

Falstaff   Well said, Hal! To it, Hal! Nay, you shall find no
75   boy's play here, I can tell you.

   [*Enter* **Douglas***; he fights with* **Falstaff***, who falls down as
   if he were dead. Exit* **Douglas***. The* **Prince** *mortally
   wounds* **Hotspur**]

Hotspur   O Harry, thou hast robbed me of my youth!
      I better brook the loss of brittle life
      Than those proud titles thou hast won of me;
      They wound my thoughts worse than thy sword my flesh:
80   But thoughts, the slaves of life, and life, time's fool,
      And time, that takes survey of all the world,
      Must have a stop. O, I could prophesy,
      But that the earthy and cold hand of death
      Lies on my tongue: no, Percy, thou art dust,
85   And food for –

                                             [*Dies*]

Prince   For worms, brave Percy. Fare thee well, great
      heart!
      Ill-weaved ambition, how much art thou shrunk!
      When that this body did contain a spirit,
      A kingdom for it was too small a bound;

Prince   I'll make it greater before I go. I'll pluck all the
feathers from your cap to make myself a garland!

Hotspur   I can't take any more of your conceit!

[*They fight*]

[**Falstaff** *enters*]

Falstaff   Well done Hal! At him Hal! No kids' stuff
here I can tell you!

[**Douglas** *enters, and fights with* **Falstaff**. **Falstaff**
falls down, pretending to be dead. **Douglas** *leaves. The*
Prince *gives* **Hotspur** *a mortal wound*]

Hotspur   Oh Harry! You've robbed me of my youth!
The loss of fragile life is easier to bear than yielding you
my battle honours. The thought of that hurts more than
your sword-thrust. But thought depends on life, and life
is at the whim of time, and time – which dominates the
world – must have a stop. Oh, I could make prophecies:
but the hand of death, cold and earthy, silences my
tongue. No, Percy. It's dust you are, and food for –
[*He dies in mid-sentence*]

Prince   – for worms, brave Percy! Farewell, great
heart! Ill-conceived amibition: to have shrunk to this!
When this body was alive, a kingdom was too small for
it. Now, six feet of vile earth is room enough. The earth

90 But now two paces of the vilest earth
Is room enough. This earth that bears thee dead
Bears not alive so stout a gentleman.
If thou wert sensible of courtesy
I should not make so dear a show of zeal;
95 But let my favours hide thy mangled face,
And even in thy behalf I'll thank myself
For doing these fair rites of tenderness.
Adieu, and take thy praise with thee to heaven!
Thy ignominy sleep with thee in the grave,
100 But not remembered in thy epitaph!

[*He spies* **Falstaff** *on the ground*]

What, old acquaintance, could not all this flesh
Keep in a little life? Poor Jack, farewell!
I could have better spared a better man:
O, I should have a heavy miss of thee
105 If I were much in love with vanity:
Death hath not struck so fat a deer today,
Though many dearer, in this bloody fray.
Embowelled will I see thee by and by,
Till then in blood by noble Percy lie.

[*Exit*]

[**Falstaff** *rises up*]

110 **Falstaff**   Embowelled? If thou embowel me today, I'll give
you leave to powder me and eat me too tomorrow.
'Sblood, 'twas time to counterfeit or that hot termagant
Scot has paid me Scot and lot too. Counterfeit? I lie; I am
no counterfeit: to die is to be a counterfeit, for he is but
the counterfeit of a man, who hath not the life of a man:
but to counterfeit dying, when a man thereby liveth, is to

on which you lie dead sustains no living man more
valiant. If you could respond to compliments, I wouldn't
be so demonstrative – but I'll cover your mangled face
with my insignia, and thank myself on your behalf for
performing this kindly ceremony. [*He removes the silk
band from his helmet; it is white and blue, the Prince's
personal colours*] Farewell, and take your praises with
you to heaven! May your shame sleep with you in the
grave but not be remembered in your epitaph. [*He sees
Falstaff lying on the ground*] What, old friend: couldn't all
this flesh retain a little life? Poor Jack, farewell! I could
have lost a better man more readily. You'd be a heavy
loss if I really loved frivolity. You're the fattest deer to die
in this bloody battle, though not the dearest! I'll have you
disembowelled by and by. Till then, lie in your blood near
noble Percy.

[*He goes*]

[**Falstaff** *gets to his feet*]

Falstaff   Disembowelled? Disembowel me today, and
I'll give you my permission to pickle and eat me, too,
tomorrow! Christ! It was time to do a bit of acting, or
that bloodthirsty Scot would have put paid to me: lock,
stock and barrel! Acting? I tell a lie. I'm no actor. To die
is to be an actor, because a man with no life is only
pretending to be a man. To sham death in order to live is
not to act. It's life in all its reality. Valour's noblest
quality is discretion; that nobility has saved my life. [*He

115   be no counterfeit, but the true and perfect image of life
indeed. The better part of valour is discretion, in the
which better part I have saved my life. 'Zounds, I am
afraid of this gunpowder Percy, though he be dead; how if
he should counterfeit too and arise? By my faith, I am

120   afraid he would prove the better counterfeit: therefore I'll
make him sure, yea, and I'll swear I killed him. Why may
not he rise as well as I? Nothing confutes me but eyes,
and nobody sees me: therefore, sirrah (*stabbing him*), with a
new wound in your thigh, come you along with me.

125   [*He takes up* **Hotspur** *on his back*]

    [*Enter* **Prince** *and* **John of Lancaster**]

Prince   Come, brother John, full bravely hast thou fleshed
Thy maiden sword.

130 **Lancaster**   But soft, whom have we here?
Did you not tell me this fat man was dead?

Prince   I did, I saw him dead,
Breathless and bleeding on the ground. Art thou alive?
Or is it fantasy that plays upon our eyesight?
I prithee speak, we will not trust our eyes

135   Without our ears: thou art not what thou seem'st.

Falstaff   No, that's certain, I am not a double-man; but if I
be not Jack Falstaff, then am I a Jack: there is Percy!
[*throwing the body down*] If your father will do me any
honour, so: if not, let him kill the next Percy himself. I

140   look to be either earl or duke, I can assure you.

Prince   Why, Percy I killed myself, and saw thee dead.

looks at the corpse at his side] Jesus, I'm scared of this gunpowder Percy, even though he's dead. What if he does some acting too, and gets up? By all that's holy, I'm afraid he'd make the better actor. Therefore I'll make sure of him. Yes, and I'll swear I killed him! What's to stop him getting up like me? Only an eye-witness could say me nay – and there's nobody here to see. Therefore, sir – [*He stabs the body*] with a new wound in your thigh, come along with me! [*He lifts* **Hotspur** *over his shoulder.*]

[*Enter the* **Prince** *and* **Lord John of Lancaster**]

Prince   Come, brother John. You've initiated your maiden sword most bravely.

Lancaster   A moment. Who's this? Didn't you tell me this fat man was dead?

Prince   I did. I saw him dead: breathless and bleeding on the ground. Are you alive? Or do our eyes deceive us? Speak, will you? We won't trust our eyes without the confirmation of our ears. You aren't what you seem . . .

Falstaff   No, that's for sure. It's not me and my double! If I'm not Jack Falstaff, then I'm a knavish sort of Jack. [*He throws* **Hotspur's** *body down*] There's Percy. If your father will grant me some honour, so be it. If not, he can kill the next Percy himself. I expect to be either an Earl or a Duke, I assure you.

Prince   Why, I killed Percy myself, and saw you dead!

¹⁴⁵ **Falstaff** Didst thou? Lord, Lord, how this world is given
to lying! I grant you I was down, and out of breath, and
so was he, but we rose both at an instant, and fought a
long hour by Shrewsbury clock. If I may be believed, so: if
not, let them that should reward valour bear the sin upon
¹⁵⁰ their own heads. I'll take it upon my death, I gave him
this wound in the thigh; if the man were alive, and would
deny it, 'zounds, I would make him eat a piece of my
sword.

Lancaster This is the strangest tale that ever I heard.

¹⁵⁵ **Prince** This is the strangest fellow, brother John.
Come, bring your luggage nobly on your back.
For my part, if a lie may do thee grace,
I'll gild it with the happiest terms I have.

[A retreat is sounded]

¹⁶⁰ The trumpet sounds retreat, the day is ours.
Come, brother, let us to the highest of the field,
To see what friends are living, who are dead.

[Exeunt **Prince of Wales** *and* **Lancaster**]

Falstaff I'll follow, as they say, for reward. He that
¹⁶⁵ rewards me, God reward him! If I do grow great, I'll grow
less, for I'll purge, and leave sack, and live cleanly as a
nobleman should do.

[Exit bearing off the body]

Falstaff   Did you? Lord, Lord! How this world is addicted to lying! I grant you I was down, and out of breath – and so was he – but we both got up together and fought for a long hour by the town clock at Shrewsbury. If I may be believed: right! If not, let those responsible for rewarding valour live with the guilt. You have my solemn oath: I gave him this wound in the thigh. If the man were alive and he denied it, Jesus! I'd make him eat a piece of my sword!

Lancaster   This is the strangest tale I ever heard!

Prince   This is the strangest fellow, brother John.
Come then. Put your luggage proudly on your back. As far as I'm concerned, if one of your lies will do you some good, I'll endorse it as warmly as I'm able.

[*A retreat is sounded*]

The trumpet sounds the retreat. We've won the day.
Come, brother, let's go to some high ground to see which friends are living, and who are dead.

[*The* **Prince** *and* **Lord John** *leave*]

Falstaff   I'll follow as they say, for the handouts. God reward the man who rewards me! Greatness will lead to smallness, because I'll repent, and give up wine, and live decently like a nobleman should do . . .

[*He departs, dragging off the body*]

Scene 5

The same. The trumpets sound. Enter the **King**, **Prince of**
Wales, Lord John of Lancaster, Earl of Westmoreland,
with **Worcester** *and* **Vernon** *prisoners*

King   Thus ever did rebellion find rebuke.
   Ill-spirited Worcester, did not we send grace,
   Pardon, and terms of love to all of you?
   And wouldst thou turn our offers contrary?
5   Misuse the tenor of thy kinsman's trust?
   Three knights upon our party slain today,
   A noble earl and many a creature else,
   Had been alive this hour,
   If like a Christian thou hadst truly borne
10   Betwixt our armies true intelligence.

Worcester   What I have done my safety urged me to;
   And I embrace this fortune patiently,
   Since not to be avoided it falls on me.

King   Bear Worcester to the death, and Vernon too:
15   Other offenders we will pause upon.

                   [*Exeunt* **Worcester** *and* **Vernon**, *guarded*]

How goes the field?

Prince   The noble Scot, Lord Douglas, when he saw
   The fortune of the day quite turned from him,
   The noble Percy slain, and all his men
20   Upon the foot of fear, fled with the rest,
   And falling from a hill, he was so bruised
   That the pursuers took him. At my tent
   The Douglas is; and I beseech your Grace
   I may dispose of him.

Scene 5

The Battlefield. Trumpets sound. Enter the **King,** *the* **Prince of Wales, Lord John of Lancaster,** *the* **Earl of Westmoreland** *with* **Worcester** *and* **Vernon** *as prisoners*

King   Rebellion, as ever, is firmly crushed. Ill-natured Worcester: did we not send clemency, pardon and messages of goodwill to you all? And did you not convey the opposite? Take advantage of your kinsman's trust? Three of our knights killed today, a noble earl, and many lesser men besides would all be living now if, like a Christian, you had faithfully reported the true reply.

Worcester   I acted as I did for safety reasons. I am resigned to my fate. I cannot avoid it.

King   Take Worcester to be executed: and Vernon too. We'll think further about the other rebels.

[**Worcester** *and* **Vernon** *are escorted out*]

How are things on the battlefield?

Prince   When that noble Scot, Lord Douglas, saw he'd lost the day, with the noble Percy killed, and all his men running off in panic, he fled with the rest. Then, falling from a hill, he was so bruised that the pursuers captured him. Douglas is at my tent. Would your Grace allow me to dispose of him?

King   With all my heart.

25 **Prince**   Then, brother John of Lancaster, to you
      This honourable bounty shall belong;
      Go to the Douglas and deliver him
      Up to his pleasure, ransomless and free:
      His valours shown upon our crests today
30   Have taught us how to cherish such high deeds,
      Even in the bosom of our adversaries.

Lancaster   I thank your Grace for this high courtesy,
      Which I shall give away immediately.

King   Then this remains, that we divide our power:
35   You, son John, and my cousin Westmoreland,
      Towards York shall bend you with your dearest speed
      To meet Northumberland and the prelate Scroop,
      Who, as we hear, are busily in arms:
      Myself and you, son Harry, will towards Wales,
40   To fight with Glendower and the Earl of March.
      Rebellion in this land shall lose his sway,
      Meeting the check of such another day,
      And since this business so fair is done,
      Let us not leave till all our own be won.

                                              [*Exeunt*]

King   With all my heart.

Prince   Well then, brother John of Lancaster, this act of charity is yours: go to Douglas and give him his freedom, without ransom or conditions. His valour against our men today has taught us how to value such courageous deeds, even when they're demonstrated by our enemies.

Lancaster   I thank your Grace for this great courtesy. I'll act upon it immediately.

King   Then only this remains. We must split our forces. You, son John, with my cousin Westmoreland, must make for York at top speed to confront Northumberland and Archbishop Scroop. Both, so we hear, are busy mobilizing. I myself, and you, son Harry, will make towards Wales to fight Glendower and the Earl of March. Another setback like this one, and rebellion will cease to be a force in this kingdom. We've done so well today, let's not rest till we've recovered all that's ours.

[*They leave*]

Activities

Characters

Search the text to find answers to the following questions. They will help you to form personal opinions about the major characters in the play. *Record any relevant quotations in Shakespeare's own words.*

King Henry IV

1   The King opens the play by referring to the past. What has been the principal feature of his reign?

2   He makes plans for a crusade.

    a What are his political motives?
    b What does this tell us about him?

3   In *Act I Scene 1*, he receives

    a good news
    b bad news
    Identify both, and comment on the King's reactions.

4   How can you tell from the same scene that he is
    a a King with problems
    b a father with problems
    c an organizer capable of dealing with problems?

5   In *Act I Scene 3* we see the King in his Council Chamber, dealing with a subject who has been described earlier as 'malevolent'.

    a In his opening speech, what does the King accuse himself of?
    b He says he will change. In what way?

c How does he put his resolution into immediate action?

d Comment on the incident as an indicator of his character and qualities.

6 In his handling of Northumberland and his son Hotspur

   a what makes him angry?

   b which of his words show that he is

      i unforgiving

      ii forthright?

7 **a** In *Act I Scene 3*, Hotspur calls Henry 'this unthankful King', 'this ingrate', 'this forgetful man', and early in the scene Worcester reveals the reason for the allegation.

      i Trace it

      ii Explain how it accounts for Henry's troubled reign.

   b Hotspur also calls him 'this subtle king', 'this vile politician', 'this king of smiles', 'this fawning greyhound'.

      i What does he mean?

      ii Which speech of Worcester's towards the end of the scene shows that he is in agreement?

8 In the speech that opens *Act III Scene 2*, there is a suggestion that the King is harbouring guilty feelings. Which lines provide the clue?

9 Read the King's speech in *Act III Scene 2* from 'Had I so lavish of my presence been' to the end. Find evidence that Henry is

   a a scheming sort of man

   b a man conscious of his own dignity and importance

   c a man who scorns weakness and self-indulgence

   d a man who assumes a false character to gain support

   e a King whose royal bearing is studied rather than natural.

10 Later in the same scene, Henry shows that he

   a admires Hotspur. For what qualities?

    b distrusts his son. Which lines of Hotspur's in *Act I Scene 3* show that others have noticed this?

11 At the end of *Act III Scene 2*, what can we deduce about
    a Henry's private information service?
    b his ability as an organizer and decision maker?

12 Read the exchange of words between Sir Walter Blunt and Hotspur in *Act IV Scene 3*, on the subject of Henry's willingness to make concessions.
    a Study Blunt's message carefully. What would be your reason for
      i trusting Henry
      ii being suspicious of him?
    b Study Hotspur's reply. How much of it might well be true?

13 **a** Read what Worcester says to the King in *Act V Scene 1*. How far do you think he is in the right, and how far in the wrong?
    b Comment on the King's 'offer of our grace', and on Worcester's reasons in *Act V Scene 2* for keeping it from Hotspur.

14 In *Act V Scene 3*, Hotspur says 'The King hath many marching in his coats'.
    a What does he mean?
    b What does this tell us about the strength of support for Henry as King?
    c Who loses his life as a consequence?

15 What do we learn of the King's character
    a in battle?
    b after it?

Prince Henry

1   **a** What impression of Prince Hal do we gain from the first references to him in the play?

    b Does his first appearance in the play confirm what has been said about him?

2   In *Act I Scene 2*, find examples of

    a Prince Hal's sense of humour

    b his skill in word-play

    c his knowledge of low life

    d his pleasure in provoking Jack Falstaff.

3   Falstaff invites the Prince to join him in a highway robbery.

    a What is the Prince's instinctive response?

    b What makes him change his mind?

    c What is his explanation for his life-style as expressed in the soliloquy at the end of *Act I Scene 2*, and what does this tell us about his character?

    d Why do you think this soliloquy is in blank verse?

4   **a** Hotspur refers to the Prince in *Act I Scene 3*. Find the quotation, comment on the truth of it, and say why Hotspur speaks as he does.

    b The Prince refers to Hotspur in *Act II Scene 4*. Look up his remarks, comment on the truth of them, and say why the Prince speaks as he does.

5   **a** Find a speech in *Act II Scene 2* which sums up in a single sentence the reason why the Prince is involved in the robbery at Gad's Hill.

    b What further evidence is there at the close of this scene that the Prince's main object is something other than money?

    c Look up the Prince's dialogues with the Sheriff at the end of *Act II Scene 4*, and with Falstaff at the end of *Act*

III *Scene 3*. Say what they tell us of the true nature of the Prince.

6 The scene in the Boar's Head Tavern after the robbery [*Act II Scene 4*] shows the Prince in the merriest of moods.

a He says he has 'sounded the very base-string of humility'. What does he say he has learned – and how does this distinguish him from his father at the same age?

b Explain the practical joke he plays on Francis.

c Explain how he obtains the maximum of fun out of Falstaff's version of the robbery.

d Give examples of the Prince's ability to use language in the style of common tavern brawlers.

7 **a** At which point in the Tavern Scene [*Act II Scene 4*] does the real world of serious politics enter into the revelry?

b How does the Prince react to the news?

c How might his drinking companions be misled by his manner at this time?

8 **a** The comedy of the play-acting in the Tavern Scene involves irreverence to the King, who is impersonated. Read the episode carefully and decide

i whether the laughter is ever at the King's expense or

ii whether the Prince is careful to see that the subject of the mockery is always Falstaff.

b What do you think is the dramatic reason why Shakespeare ends this episode

i at 'I do, I will', and

ii with knocking and the excited entry of Bardolph?

c How does the mood of the Prince change after the entry of the Sheriff? Give examples of his responsible manner.

9 The confrontation between the King and the Prince in *Act III Scene 2* is as solemn as the mock interview in *Act II Scene 4* was hilarious:

a List the many reasons why the King is displeased with his son.

b Which words, spoken by the Prince in *Act I Scene 2*, are here put to the test?

c Which words, spoken by the Prince in *Act III Scene 2*, show that he is prepared to honour his earlier resolution?

d Which words of the King prompt the Prince to progress from a promise to a vow?

e Father and son express the intensity of their feelings in terms of a number. What is it?

10 The King grants the Prince 'charge and sovereign trust'. When we see Hal next, in *Act III Scene 3*, he is at the Boar's Head Tavern again.

a How does the Prince's handling of the Hostess/Falstaff quarrel accord with his promise to behave responsibly?

b How does he handle the outstanding matter of the robbery?

c How does he handle Falstaff's suggestion about robbing the Exchequer?

d How does he show that he is capable of carrying the responsibility that the King has given him?

11 a Find Hotspur's reference to the Prince in *Act IV Scene 1*, and

b find the Prince's reference to Hotspur in *Act V Scene 1*. At this stage of the play, which seems most to the speaker's credit, and why?

12 Compare the Prince's manner with Falstaff before the battle [*Act IV Scene 3*] and that during it [*Act V Scene 3*]. How do the two scenes illustrate his wide behavioural range?

13 In *Act V Scene 4*, the Prince is in the thick of the battle.

a At what point is the King totally convinced of his son's reformation?

    b What is the evidence that he is a courageous soldier?

    c What is the evidence that he can be generous in praise of worthy allies?

    d What is the evidence that he can be generous in praise of worthy enemies?

    e What evidence is there that he can be generous in praise of entertaining rogues?

    f What evidence is there that he is modest with regard to his personal achievements?

14 In the last scene of the play [*Act V Scene 5*] the Prince performs two generous acts.

    a What are they?

    b Which of them might indicate a shrewd political wisdom?

Hotspur

1   **a** At the beginning of the play, Hotspur enjoys an enviable reputation. From the King's reference to him in *Act I Scene 1*, establish what this is.

    b How does the Prince's jocular reference to him in *Act II Scene 4* act as confirmation?

2   Hotspur speaks for himself in *Act I Scene 3*. Look up his description of the scene of battle at Holmedon, and show how it reveals

    a his valour and manliness

    b his short temper

    c his capacity for mockery.

3   **a** In *Act I Scene 3*, why is Hotspur at cross-purposes with the King, and what word in particular goads him into an angry outburst?

    b What do we learn from this exchange of words of Hotspur's behaviour when provoked?

c Which of his words show him to be impulsive and rash?

d What evidence is there that Worcester and Northumberland know how to lead him on?

e What evidence is there that having been led on, Hotspur is unstoppable in his passion: 'wasp-stung and impatient'?

f What is Hotspur's attitude to flatterers?

g What is Hotspur's attitude to honour?

4 **a** At the opening of *Act II Scene 3*, Hotspur is alone, reading a letter, and commenting on its contents. What do we learn of his character from his remarks?

    b   i What do we learn of his relationship with his wife Kate from their dialogue in this scene?

        ii What further evidence is there in *Act III Scene 1*?

5 **a** Hotspur's first words in *Act III Scene 1*, in which the rebels meet to discuss their plans, are typical of him: why?

    b What is typical about his first exchanges with Owen Glendower?

    c What does Mortimer realize that Hotspur does not?

6 The first business of the meeting is to agree on new territorial boundaries.

    a Why does Hotspur object to the Archbishop's plan?

    b Is his proposed revision reasonable?

    c How does he come to clash with Glendower yet again?

    d What is characteristic of Hotspur's attitude once Glendower has backed down?

    e What is revealing about Hotspur's attitude to poetry as expressed in this dispute?

    f What is revealing about Hotspur's explanation for his dislike of Glendower?

    g Which words of Worcester's sum up the reasons why Hotspur's behaviour needs improvement?

7 Two key words stand out in the dialogue between Hotspur and Douglas which opens *Act IV Scene 1*.

    a What are they?

    b Comment on their relevance to an understanding of Hotspur's character.

8 Comment on

    a Hotspur's initial reaction to the news of his father's sickness and

    b his second thoughts and his supporting arguments.

    What do the latter tell us of his thought processes?

9 Comment on

    a Hotspur's response to Sir Richard Vernon's first announcement.

    b Hotspur's response to Sir Richard Vernon's second piece of news.

    c Hotspur's response to praise of Prince Henry.

10 From the evidence of the closing speeches of *Act IV Scene 1* decide

    a what is Hotspur's instinctive reaction to bad news and

    b whether he is confident of victory.

11 *Act IV Scene 3* opens with a quarrel; Hotspur has taken up a fixed point of view.

    a What is it?

    b Why is it typical of him?

12 Sir Walter Blunt invites Hotspur to name his grievances.

    a What is the nature of Hotspur's reply?

    b Why does Blunt say 'I came not to hear this'?

    c What is significant about Hotspur's postponement of a decision?

13 **a** Look up the reasons why Worcester decides not to pass on the 'liberal kind offer of the King' [*Act V Scene 2*].

To what extent does he correctly portray his nephew?

b Consider Hotspur's first question on hearing of Prince Hal's challenge. Why is the answer important to him?

c The answer provokes a significant comment. How does it distinguish Hotspur's character from that of Prince Hal?

d Twice in this scene Hotspur professes to be no talker. Find his words, and decide whether he is right about himself.

e What is significant about the way in which Hotspur deals with the Messenger who comes with letters?

14 In *Act V Scene 4*, the two Harrys meet in battle.

a By what name does Harry Percy address his adversary?

b In what name does Harry Monmouth reply?

c Which of the two men is the more courteous?

15 **a** What most concerns Hotspur in his dying moments?

b What qualities does the Prince emphasize in his valediction?

c Compare the Prince's references to Hotspur from this point in the play with Falstaff's reference to him. Are the two incompatible?

Falstaff

1 **a** The banter between the Prince and Falstaff in *Act I Scene 2* contains a catalogue of references to the latter's vices. List as many of them as you can find.

b Select examples of Falstaff's
  i skill in word-play
  ii skill in punning
  iii skill in turning vice into apparent virtue.

c Why is Falstaff's roguish way of life amusing here rather than reprehensible?

d How do his drinking companions use Falstaff's
  i girth,
  ii immoral behaviour and
  iii proneness to lying as sources of merriment?

2 At the scene of the Gad's Hill robbery, [*Act I Scene 2*], Falstaff is, as usual, the butt of insults and jokes.

  a Read his soliloquy at the beginning of the scene, and the dialogue immediately following. Choose examples of
    i comic exaggeration
    ii comic explanation
    iii comic self-criticism
    iv comic oaths and insults
    v comic threats

  b The ambush of the travellers is taken by Falstaff as an opportunity for further outrageous fun. Explain the preposterousness of
    i his allusions to age
    ii his allusions to fatness.

  c Why is cowardice so amusing in this scene?

3 Cowardice is the prevailing theme of Falstaff's protests when we see him next in *Act II Scene 4*. He repeatedly and emphatically denounces it.

  a How does his response to Poins's aggressiveness turn self-righteousness into comedy?

  b Trace the comic element in Falstaff's narrative account of the Gad's Hill robbery. Identify his
    i boasts
    ii lies
    iii exaggerations
    iv evasions
    v excuses
    vi devious tricks.

4 In the play-acting episode in *Act II Scene 4*, Falstaff shows great comic versatility when pretending to be the King.

    a He parodies the ranting style of theatrical performance. Which lines are intended to sound like 'one of these harlotry players'?

    b He pretends to be pious. Which of his words sound like a sermon?

    c He mixes solemnity with buffoonery. Explain how he does this

       i when giving reasons for his 'son's' probable legitimacy

      ii when turning the subject round to the company Henry is said to keep

     iii when referring to himself.

5 When pretending to be the Prince, Falstaff is

    a comically innocent. Which line shows that he knows how to handle the Prince's eloquent abuse?

    b touchingly defensive. Examine his last speech before being cut short by Bardolph's entry. How much of what he says has a ring of pathos and seriousness about it?

6 While 'fast asleep behind the arras', Falstaff's pockets are searched by Peto. Comment on the contents.

7 Falstaff's final appearance in the Boar's Head Tavern prior to the Battle of Shrewsbury, [*Act III Scene 3*], finds him, according to Bardolph, in a 'fretful' mood.

    a His opening speech to Bardolph contains several familiar Falstaffian themes: identify them.

    b His second speech shows that he has not lost his sense of humour. How does he cleverly choose his words to comic effect?

    c In his exchange of verbal wit with Bardolph over their physical appearances, why is Falstaff the clear winner?

d What is characteristically roguish about his dialogue with the Hostess, and his exchanges with the Prince?

e What evidence is there that the Prince's trust in Falstaff as a military man is misplaced?

8 In *Act IV Scene 2*, Falstaff stops for refreshment and speaks of his 'misuse of the King's press'.

a What do we learn from this of Elizabethan methods of recruitment?

b What do we learn of Falstaff's unscrupulousness?

9 **a** Falstaff is present in *Act V Scene 1* when Worcester meets the King at his camp near Shrewsbury. Explain why the Prince silences him after his one contribution to this summit meeting.

b Left alone at the end of this scene, Falstaff soliloquises on the theme of Honour. What is his attitude to it, and how is it characteristic?

10 In *Act V Scene 3* Falstaff is present at the Battle of Shrewsbury. Examine

a his further remarks on the theme of Honour, and

b his dialogue with the Prince and identify examples of his roguery.

11 Falstaff's adventures on the battlefield are further depicted in *Act V Scene 4*.

a How is his conduct in the encounter with Douglas consistent with his philosophy and character?

b In what ways does the Prince's valediction identify the essence of Falstaff's appeal as a human being?

c Falstaff's resurrection, subsequent actions, and dialogue with the King's sons show him to be incorrigible. Analyse these examples of Falstaffian clowning.

12 Falstaff's last words in the play are in the form of a short soliloquy. What is familiar about the sentiments he expresses?

Owen Glendower

1   In *Act II Scene 1*, Glendower makes certain claims which
    cause Hotspur to say 'there's no man speaks better Welsh'.
    a What are the claims?
    b What does Hotspur mean?

2   **a** What further claims does Glendower make which sug-
    gest he is no mere braggart?
    b Why is Hotspur's comment on them provocative?

3   **a** What evidence is there in *Act II Scene 1* to show that
    Glendower is willing to control his feelings for the sake
    of unity?
    b What evidence is there to show that Hotspur is not?

4   **a** In the same scene Hotspur says Glendower is 'tedious'.
    What examples does he give of this aspect of
    Glendower's character?
    b Mortimer defends Glendower. What does he say are his
    virtues?

5   What evidence is there of
    a Glendower's tender understanding of women?
    b his love of music?

Worcester

1   In *Act I Scene 1*, Westmoreland identifies Worcester as the
    King's enemy. What does he accuse him of?

2   We first see Worcester in *Act I Scene 3*.
    a Why does he give immediate offence to the King?
    b What does the King detect in his manner?
    c How does Worcester
       i   provoke Hotspur to anger against Henry?
       ii show that he is indeed plotting to overthrow the
           King?
       iii justify his actions?

3 In *Act III Scene 1*, Worcester speaks once to support Hotspur in his argument, and once to censure him.

   a What does this suggest about Worcester's political methods?

   b What does this tell us of his understanding of Hotspur?

4 Worcester puts his case for involvement in the rebellion in *Act V Scene 1*.

   a What is his complaint?

   b What is the King's response?

5 In *Act V Scene 2*, we learn Worcester's private opinion of the King's offer to Hotspur.

   a What is it?

   b Why does he suppress it?

6 In *Act V Scene 5*, the King sends Worcester to his death.

   a What is the King's declared reason for calling him 'ill-spirited'?

   b Is Worcester's reply consistent with the facts?

Structure

1   The play has both a main and a sub-plot.

    a Which characters appear in both?

    b The sub-plot is in prose, except for a soliloquy, which is in verse. Find this exception to the rule, and explain it.

2   In the main plot, Hotspur and the Prince are contrasted.

    a Find the speech in *Act I Scene 1* which sums up the differences in their characters

    b Find scenes (or parts of scenes) which demonstrate
        i   Hotspur at his most valiant
        ii   The Prince at his most valiant
        iii   Hotspur at his most irresponsible
        iv   The Prince at his most irresponsible
        v   Hotspur in a good humour
        vi   The Prince in a good humour
        vii   Hotspur angry
        viii   The Prince angry
        ix   Hotspur acting hot-headedly
        x   The Prince acting with calm dignity
        xi   Hotspur acting arrogantly
        xii   The Prince acting modestly
        xiii   Hotspur acting generously towards a friend
        xiv   The Prince acting generously towards a friend
        xv   Hotspur speaking slightingly of an enemy
        xvi   The Prince speaking favourably of an enemy
        xvii   Hotspur acting intolerantly
        xviii   The Prince acting tolerantly

3   **a** In the main plot, Hotspur speaks about Honour.
        i   Find the relevant speeches
        ii   Explain Hotspur's attitude to Honour
        iii   Give an example of his philosophy in practice.

    b In the sub-plot, Falstaff also speaks about Honour
      i Find the relevant speeches
      ii Explain his attitude to Honour
      iii Give an example of his philosophy in practice.

4   In the main and the sub plots

    a Age and Youth are contrasted. In what ways?
    b Law and law-breaking are contrasted. Explain how.
    c Heroism and cowardice are contrasted. Give examples.
    d Vice and virtue are contrasted. In which characters?
    e Nobles and commoners are contrasted. What seem to be the pre-occupations of each?
    f Respect for human life and disregard for human life are contrasted. Who shows the former, and who the latter?

Textual questions

Read the original Shakespeare and (if necessary) the modern transcription, to gain an understanding of the speeches and extracts below. Then concentrate entirely on the original in answering the questions.

1   *So shaken as we are, so wan with care* [*Act I Scene 1*]

   a In this speech there are a number of references to physical discomfort and disorder. Find them.

   b What three unnatural and undesirable experiences does the King say the soil of England has experienced?

   c Identify examples of
      i   personification
      ii simile
      iii metaphor
   and say how they contribute to the effectiveness of the speech.

2   *I know you all, and will awhile uphold* [*Act I Scene 2*]

   a Why is the Prince's soliloquy in blank verse, whereas the rest of the scene is in prose?

   b Which words in the second line convey his contempt for his companions' way of life?

   c How does he use a comparison with the sun and the clouds to explain his present conduct?

   d How does he use reference to work and play to justify his plans?

   e How does contrast ('how much' – 'so much') give scale to his reformation?

   f Explain how the use of simile enables the Prince to explain his strategy.

   g What is gained by having the last two lines rhyme?

3 *My liege, I did deny no prisoners* [*Act I Scene 3*]

   a The first line is a dogmatic statement. The lines that follow are a vivid reconstruction of an incident after the Battle of Holmedon. At what point does Hotspur begin to bring his narrative statement to life?

   b At this point, Hotspur introduces several similes. How effective are they in conveying the character of the man he is describing?

   c Why does Hotspur go into such fine detail over the 'certain lord's' use of the pouncet box?

   d Which lines suggest that Hotspur is mocking and impersonating the unwelcome lord?

   e Hotspur says he is 'pestered with a popinjay'. Why is this an effective way of referring to the King's messenger?

   f Why does Hotspur use the expression 'God save the mark'?

   g How does Hotspur ridicule the messenger's empty-headedness?

4 *Revolted Mortimer?*
He never did fall off, my sovereign liege, [*Act I Scene 3*]

   a This is a passionate, emotional speech. How does repetition give Hotspur's words an emotive force?

   b Which words describe the gentleness of nature?

   c Which words describe the brutality of combat?

   d What is gained by contrasting the two?

5 *Nay, then I cannot blame his cousin King* [*Act I Scene 3*]

   a Here, Hotspur is eloquently persuasive in making out a case against the King. How many times does he refer to him, and what adjectives does he use to show his dislike?

   b i After his initial statement, Hotspur asks a series of rhetorical questions. How does the repetition of 'shall it –' convey his intense feelings?

    ii Which word answers his own questions, and is the climax of the appeal to his listeners?

c Explain the effectiveness of Hotspur's series of words which begins with 'agents' and ends with 'hangman'.

d How does Hotspur play upon pride, honour, and public opinion to sway his father and Worcester?

e Hotspur uses a very effective horticultural image. Identify it and say why it is so well-chosen.

6   *By heaven, methinks it were an easy leap* [*Act I Scene 3*]

    a What is the effect of Hotspur's opening exclamation?

    b What is the effect of the contrasting adjectives in line two?

    c How does reference to 'the moon' on the one hand, and 'the deep' on the other, give heroic scale to Hotspur's boast?

    d How does personification add to Hotspur's claim to be a man of honour?

7   *I am accursed to rob in that thief's company* [*Act II Scene 2*]

    a Cursing and swearing oaths is common in the prose scenes.

       i What is the justification for this?

      ii How many examples can you find, and what are the most frequent themes?

    b Whereas in court society men address each other politely, in the Tavern scenes they do not. What terms of abuse are used here?

    c Lawlessness and punishment pre-occupy the minds of Falstaff and his low-life companions. What examples are there in this passage?

    d Falstaff often pretends he is the victim of conspiracies to corrupt or influence him. What is the instance of this here?

    e Colloquial expressions and exclamations are a notable feature of Falstaff's speeches. What are the examples in this passage?

f Falstaff is given to exaggeration.

    i Where does he indulge in it in this speech?

    ii What is his purpose?

8 *God pardon thee! Yet let me wonder, Harry* [*Act III Scene 3*]

a In this lengthy indictment the King begins by accusing the Prince of deviating from the standards of his ancestors. He uses an image to express this. Explain its probable source and say whether it is effective.

b He then proceeds to list the Prince's shortcomings. What are the four sources of his dissatisfaction?

c The King compares the Prince's conduct with his own.

    i What is the essential difference between their lifestyles?

    ii Which words convey the King's disapproval?

d What does the use of direct speech – 'This is he'; 'Where, which is Bolingbroke?' – add to the force of the King's indictment?

e The three verbs 'stole', 'dressed' and 'pluck' have been admired for the way in which they enliven the narrative here. Explain why.

f The King uses two similes to describe his 'presence'. Explain how each reinforces his argument about keeping aloof.

g i In expressing contempt for his predecessor (Richard II) and his acquaintances, the King uses a number of highly effective adjectives. Comment on them.

    ii Note the King's choice of verbs. How do they, too, convey the King's scorn?

h In the Book of Proverbs it says 'If thou findest honey, eat so much as is sufficient for thee, lest thou be overfull.' Which words of the King on the same subject have a proverbial ring about them, and why?

i The sense of sight is central to the King's final words in this speech.

    i Which words are related to dullness?

    ii Which words are related to brightness?

   iii Which words are related to fatigue?

   iv Which words are related to the emotions?

9 *All furnished, all in arms* [*Act IV Scene 1*]

  a This vivid descriptive speech opens with a repetition of the word 'all'. How does this help to convey the speaker's feelings of admiration for the King's army?

  b Birds and animals are central to the imagery. Examine the references carefully, and say how each contributes to the richness of the passage.

  c How does the speaker convey the colourful splendour of the scene by means of similes?

  d Which words seem charged with energy?

  e Which words in particular describe the skill and effortlessness of Prince Henry's horsemanship?

  f Editors and critics have argued over several words and their meanings in this passage.

     i 'Estridges' can mean either 'ostriches' or 'goshawks'. Ostriches are well known for their plumage which is consistent with 'All plumed like estridges'. Goshawks are associated with aggressiveness, which fits in with 'like eagles . . . .' Which interpretation do you favour?

    ii One respected editor thought 'with the wind' (line 2) was a misprint for 'wring the wind'. Consider both alternatives and say which you think suits the description best.

   iii 'Bated' is sometimes printed 'baited', and therefore can mean two things. 'To bate' is a falconry term meaning 'to flutter the wings'. 'To bait' means 'to be refreshed'. Which seems most suitable here?

10 *Ill-weaved ambition, how much art thou shrunk* [*Act V Scene 5*]

  a Hotspur's personal ambition is here compared with a

273

textile. Explain

   i 'ill-weaved' and 'shrunk' in their literal meanings

   ii 'ill-weaved' as it applies to Hotspur's ambition

   iii 'shrunk' as it applies to Hotspur personally.

b How does this opening observation relate to

   i Hotspur in life

   ii Hotspur in death?

c In what other way does the Prince contrast life and death in this passage?

d What other contrasts can you find in this passage, before the Prince sees Falstaff on the ground?

e What are the two meanings of 'better' in the Prince's valediction over his body?

f 'Heavy' has two meanings here. What are they?

g 'Dearer' has two meanings. What are they, and how is the word used in a punning sense?

11 Elizabethan England is vividly depicted in the prose scenes. What can be learned from them about

  a tavern life?

  b morality?

  c law and order?

  d punishment?

  e travel?

  f clothes?

  g working people?

  h food and drink?

  i the recruitment system?

12 Falstaff pretends to be the King in *Act II Scene 4*; this is one example of many where one character satirizes another in style and delivery.

  a Find one where Hotspur indulges in parody, and another where

  b the Prince mocks the speech and idioms of the lower classes.

Examination questions

The following are typical of the kind of examination questions set by the major examining boards:

1   Show how Hotspur acts as a foil to Prince Henry throughout the play.

2   How far is Prince Henry shown to be possessed of true nobility of character by a) his own speeches and actions and b) the speeches of other characters in the play?

3   How does Shakespeare succeed in making such an immoral man as Falstaff attractive to us?

4   What part does Honour play in *Henry IV Part One*?

5   The comic and the serious threads of *Henry IV Part One* come together in the scenes at the Battle of Shrewsbury. How successfully are they fused?

6   'The play is about leadership, honour and anarchy.' How far do you agree with this comment on *Henry IV Part One*?

7   Show how Shakespeare gives each rebel leader a distinct character, referring to any one scene in which they come together.

8   'In *Henry IV Part One*, chronicle history is little more than a tapestry hanging – which serves as a background to groups of living personages.' Do you agree that the historical element in the play is relatively insignificant?

9   Illustrate from the Tavern scenes the ability of Falstaff to extricate himself from difficult situations.

10 Compare and contrast the characters of King Henry and his son the Prince.

11 'Falstaff may be unscrupulous, but he is always either likeable or amusing or both.' Do you agree?

12 'All the rebels in the play are either fools or knaves.' Is this a fair comment?

13 What is the dramatic interest of the scene in Act III, which takes place in Wales, when the rebel leaders meet in council together?

14 Choose any two or three soliloquies, and show how they reveal the characters of the speakers.

15 Which have you found to be the more interesting: the Tavern scenes involving Falstaff, or the political scenes involving the leaders of the rebellion?

16 'Falstaff and his companions are frank and honest about their lies, whereas the court and the royal family are not.' With reference to at least two incidents and/or characters, say how far you agree.

17 How is Hotspur's character revealed in his behaviour to a) his friends, b) his wife, c) his enemies?

18 'Prince Henry and Falstaff are, at first sight, unlikely companions, but each can be said to need the other.' To what extent is this true?

19 Choose any two of the following minor characters in *Henry IV Part One* and say what their importance is to the play as a whole: a) Owen Glendower, b) Douglas, c) Worcester.

20 'The major themes of *Henry IV Part One* are all suggested in the first scene.' Illustrate and discuss.

21 'Each character has a speech and a style of his own.' Examine the truth of this statement with reference to Hotspur, Falstaff and Glendower.

22 How far does Prince Henry show true nobility of character in terms of a) his own speeches and actions and b) the speeches of other characters in the play?

23 Illustrate from the speeches of Hotspur and Glendower their emotional temperaments and use of poetic imagery.

24 Consider *Henry IV Part One* either a) as a picture of Elizabethan life or b) a play dealing with English history.

25 'Hotspur and the Prince are both chivalrous, but the Prince's is the nobler kind of chivalry.' Discuss.

26 Comment fully on Falstaff's speech and conduct after joining the King's army.

27 What are the reasons for King Henry's troubled reign, as expressed by the discontented nobles?

28 In what ways do women play a small but important role in *Henry IV Part One*?

29 'A liar and a hypocrite.' What evidence is there to support this serious charge against King Henry?

30 How are the main and the sub-plot of *Henry IV Part One* dramatically and thematically related?

One-word-answer quiz

1   What was the family motto of the Percy family?

2   What did Falstaff carry in his pistol case at the Battle of Shrewsbury?

3   Who delivered the pardon to Douglas after the Battle of Shrewsbury?

4   From which county did the rebel Mortimer recruit his army?

5   How many of his men were killed by Glendower's forces?

6   Who first pretended to be the King at the Battle of Shrewsbury, and was killed by Douglas?

7   Who next pretended to be the King and suffered the same fate?

8   Who married Glendower's daughter?

9   What was the name of Hotspur's dog?

10   Who was said to have been proclaimed heir to the throne by King Richard II?

11   What was the value of the sugar that Francis gave the Prince?

12   How many more years had Francis to serve in his apprenticeship?

13   What kind of suits were supposedly worn by Falstaff's fictitious attackers?

14   These men were reinforced by others. What was the colour of their suits?

15   On what day of the week did King Henry meet the Council at Windsor?

16   On what day did the Battle of Holmedon take place?

17   What was the name of Hotspur's Scottish ally in that battle?

18 How many knights were killed there?

19 How many hundred marks were stolen from the travellers at Gad's Hill?

20 For how many months had the King been planning his journey to the Holy Land?

21 In the rebels' division of the kingdom, whose was to be the area north of the Trent?

22 Where did King Henry first land on his return from banishment?

23 Which Archbishop sent messages to the Lord Marshal and his cousin Scroop?

24 At which town in Richard's time did Henry swear an oath that he was in England to claim the Dukedom of Lancaster and nothing more?

25 How much did Falstaff owe the Hostess for bread?

26 On which river bank did Glendower fight with Mortimer?

27 How many times did they pause for breath during the encounter?

28 In which part of the body did Falstaff wound Hotspur?

29 What did Gadshill wish to borrow from the Carrier?

30 What does Falstaff say is 'the better part of valour'?

31 Which lord acted as hostage while Worcester visited the King before the battle?

32 In which part of London was the Boar's Head Tavern?

33 On what day of the month did Douglas meet the rebels at Shrewsbury?

34 How many shirts did the Hostess say she bought for Falstaff?

35 How many pounds did she say Falstaff owed her?

36 Who acted as messenger of the King before the Battle of Shrewsbury?

37 What was a certain Lord holding between his finger and his thumb at Holmedon?

38 What, according to this person, was the best treatment for an internal bruise?

39 In which castle did Richard II's uncle, the Duke of York, live?

40 To what destination in London was the second carrier taking his load of bacon and ginger?

41 What kind of horse did Hotspur say would be his throne?

42 What did Falstaff say was 'a mere scutcheon'?

43 What part of Bardolph's anatomy did Falstaff say reminded him of hell fire?

44 Which rebel Earl did Hotspur offer to surrender to the King?

45 How many men were said to be in the King's army at Shrewsbury?

46 How many 'tattered prodigals' did Falstaff have in his company of soldiers?

47 Through which county did the King order the Prince to march en route for Shrewsbury?

48 Where did Falstaff and his men rob the pilgrims who were bound for Canterbury?

49 What kind of bird did Hotspur say he would train to say 'Mortimer!'?

50 In whose eye did King Henry see danger and disobedience?

What's missing?

Complete the following:

1   I'll so offend, to make offence a skill . . .
2   By heaven, methinks . . .
3   There is a devil haunts thee in the likeness of an old fat man . . .
4   This is the deadly spite that angers me . . .
5   A hundred thousand rebels die in this . . .
6   A son who is the theme . . .
7   The skipping King, he ambled up and down . . .
8   All furnished, all in arms; All . . .
9   Why, Hal, 'tis my vocation, Hal, . . .
10 Come, let us take a muster speedily . . .
11 I'll have a starling shall be taught to speak . . .
12 Methinks my moiety, north from Burton here . . .
13 To the latter end of a fray, and the beginning of a feast . . .
14 Falstaff sweats to death, And . . .
15 For treason is but trusted as the fox . . .
16 At my birth, The frame and huge foundation of the earth . . .
17 The land is burning, Percy stands on high . . .
18 To put down Richard, that sweet lovely rose, and . . .
19 Tomorrow, good Sir Michael, is a day wherein . . .
20 O monstrous! but one halfpennyworth of bread to . . .
21 Do thou amend thy face, and . . .
22 I know you all, and . . .
23 I do not think a braver gentleman . . .
24 Eight yards of uneven ground is . . .

25 The King is kind, and well we know the King . . .

26 No more, no more! Worse than the sun in March . . .

27 Company, villainous company, hath . . .

28 Thou hast the most unsavoury similes, and art indeed . . .

29 I tell thee what, Hal, if I tell thee a lie, . . .

30 Swear me Kate, like a lady as thou art . . .

31 The better part of valour . . .

32 Cousin, I think thou art enamoured On his follies . . .

33 If all the year were playing holidays, . . .

34 I had rather be a kitten and cry 'mew' . . .

35 Ill-weaved ambition . . .!

36 I better brook the loss of brittle life, Than . . .

37 If he outlive the envy of this day, England . . .

38 I saw young Harry with his beaver on . . .

39 If reasons were as plentiful as blackberries, I . . .

40 By God, I cannot flatter, I do defy . . .

41 Honour is . . . and so ends my catechism

42 I care not for thee, Kate; this is no world To . . .

43 A mad fellow met me on the way, and said . . .

44 O, he is as tedious As a tired horse . . .

45 Tut, tut, good enough to toss, food for powder . . .

46 I am not yet of Percy's mind, the Hotspur of the north, he that . . .

47 Do not think so, you shall not find it so; . . .

48 A goodly portly man, i'faith, and a corpulent . . .

49 I shall hereafter, my thrice gracious lord . . .

50 So shaken are we . . .

More plays in the
SHAKESPEARE MADE EASY/series

All these plays are available from your bookshop or newsagent or you can order them direct. Just tick the titles you want and complete the order form below.

_____	MACBETH	**£1.95**
_____	ROMEO AND JULIET	**£1.95**
_____	THE MERCHANT OF VENICE	**£1.95**
_____	JULIUS CAESAR	**£1.95**
_____	HENRY IV PART ONE	**£1.95**
_____	A MIDSUMMER NIGHT'S DREAM	**£1.95**

Available Spring 1985

_____	THE TEMPEST	**£2.25**
_____	TWELFTH NIGHT	**£2.25**

ARROW BOOKS, BOOKSERVICE BY POST, PO BOX 29, DOUGLAS, ISLE OF MAN, BRITISH ISLES

Please enclose a cheque or postal order made out to Arrow Books Limited for the amount due including 10p per book for postage and packing for orders within the UK.

Please print clearly

Name _____

Address _____

Whilst every effort is made to keep prices down and to keep popular books in print, Arrow Books cannot guarantee that prices will be the same as those advertised here or that the books will be available.
This applies to orders from the UK only. Overseas customers should order direct from: The Export Dept, Hutchinson House, 17/21 Conway Street, London W1P 6JD.